My Maniacal Muse

My Maniacal Muse

Dorinda Wheeler

authorHOUSE®

AuthorHouse™ LLC
1663 Liberty Drive
Bloomington, IN 47403
www.authorhouse.com
Phone: 1-800-839-8640

Published by AuthorHouse   06/10/2014

ISBN: 978-1-4969-1873-4 (sc)
ISBN: 978-1-4969-1874-1 (e)

IN LOVING MEMORY OF,

MY PARENTS:

HARRY B. WHEELER, JR. 01/24/36 - 02/15/08

&

MARGARET C. WHEELER - 10/04/37 - 06/10/10

Special thanks to: Gina Strika, C. Mack Crawley

Nicole Delorenzo and Mariana Whitaker-Ritter

Contents

Stand Tall (For Travis)

Was it not yesterday you learned to talk,
and with baby steps you began to walk?
Before my eyes an evolving young man
The world your playground, leave prints in the sand

Forever my baby, I'm so damned proud
With exaltation, stand tall in the crowd
Among elite,defend our native land
Always your dream, it's what you planned

As you embark and sail from sea to sea
Know you're loved by our family
Prayers to Great Spirit for a safe return
Now and always home fires shall burn

Before my eyes an evolving young man
The world your playground, leave prints in the sand...

Forces of Nature

Bound by love for eternity
Forces of nature, adversity
Young and exquisite in their prime
Their sins of flesh, sovereign crime

Perfectly opposite, yin yang
But when together, angels sang
Like the owl, stealthy in flight
Ideal predators out of sight

A winters eve with snow so white
Crystalline, china doll bright
Rouge stained like a Geisha's smile
Void corpses cast in a pile

Swift and accurate was their bite
Feeding on vagrants in the night
Ruby droplets a top the drift
Evidence dappled near their crypt

Sightly monsters, a perfect storm
Paradoxical in this form
Depraved snow flakes, a certainty
Bound by love for eternity...

One More Hour...

On this bench by the sea
I'd tell you just how much
You meant to me
Mom, I love you,
A woman wise
I'd give anything
To see your eyes...

Emerald Eyes...

---◦⟨⋄⟩◦---

Eyes of emerald, so raw
In them is the light you saw
Change color like Autumn leaves
Gazing brilliance in the breeze
They, the mirror to my soul
Reading between the lines, your goal
Enchanting, delightful green
Fill me up 'til I'm serene...

Just for Today

There are no promises, just today
Let me be humble in all I say
A little girl who's willing to play

Hold my head high and face all fears
Let go of all those grievous years
May I shed only joyous tears

Yesterday's gone, no tomorrow
I can not beg, steal, or borrow
Today I'm blithe, hold the sorrow

I shall grant an infectious smile
Advancing with grace and with style
Be sure life is worth my while

Just for today, I'll free my mind
Release demons, to leave them behind
Then open my heart, for love to find....

Once Upon A Time

Once my best friend, lover too
Yet today, I don't even know you
Along the way we grew far apart
All your lies have pierced my heart

Like getting shot by a shotgun shell
Being with you has been a living hell
Where do you get this feeling of entitlement?
All you deserve is shoes of cement

Tossed in the sea for shark bait
The pain you've caused doesn't compensate
There was a time when you treated me right
Now each conversation becomes a fight

The sun doesn't shine down on us anymore
Dark clouds prevail, the rain will pour
Your anger is a storm that rages on
I miss the warmth of the sun cast upon

So much history, I still have love for you
Though it's irrational, the wrong point of view
There's times I wish we could take it all back
Try to forget the pain, cut some slack

But it won't work, there's been too much rage
The chapter is over, turn the page
I can't entertain being your friend
This fairytale's over, it's the end…

'Til Death Do Us Part...

Many, many years have gone by
Since an aging doctor was mystified
An evil spell he would have cast
But the eye of his affection would not last

She was young and beautiful but very ill
A complication from forcing his will
He built a mausoleum just for her
Late each night he would enter

Rumor has it two voices were heard
People swore it was them, though she was unable to say a word
The doctor insisted they visited each and every night
Her spirit came to him, she was a lovely sight

Appearing dressed in a veil and a wedding dress
Nuptials would take place, he confessed
A Voodoo Priestess performed unholy matrimony
This priestess was paid quite well for her secrecy

The tale is told the doctor brought home his new wife
Why would this mad-man want a woman with no life?
The story goes he brought her coffin home late one night
An unseen onlooker said it was a terrible sight

Not long after, her family found out what happened to her
They notified the law, and she was found for sure
Her corpse in a wedding dress, laying in his bed
The officials found he was making love to the dead!

One Good Man

My lonely heart beats for the sound of another
The only men in my life are my son's and brother
It's been too long since I've whispered, "I love you"
I can't help but to feel so damned blue

All my days are rainy, the sun won't rise
At night the stars don't shine, only cloudy skies
Tear stained cheeks as saline rivers run down my face
I'm a fish out of water, completely out of place

I'd rather not spend the rest of my life alone
There was a time I lived it like a rolling stone
I learned early on not to trust at face value
My past haunts my present, what am I to do?

If only my life was full of serendipity
I suppose a world like that was not meant for me
They say love only comes when you do not look
It's not like I have a door shingle hanging from a hook

Back in the day, men were lined up at my door
Many moons ago, it doesn't happen anymore
Now I'd be happy to find one good man
Why they're so hard to find, I don't understand!

A Demon In Bed

She went antiquing one day to buy a brass bed
"Something extra comes with this", the proprietor said
Dark shadows and black mists began to pursue
From the very beginning, she didn't know what to do

She realized that she paid too high of a price
Whatever was in her home was not very nice
Awakening to something climbing into the bed
Shaped like a man, with a goat-like head

In a low, deep voice it said, "You'll have sex with me"
The demon raked his claws all over her body
It smelled so vile, like it never once showered
Too scared to scream, she was completely overpowered

It raped her unmercifully the very first night
Barely feasible, she endured a hell of a fright
She was bruised, scratched and bloody from head to toe
The Incubus Demon made her look like a freak show

After one night of horror, she wasn't second guessing
She acquired a priest to perform a complete house blessing
Then vowed to God she'd buy only new things
Never again would she purchase something with "strings"

Of course, she removed the old haunted bed
The priest couldn't kill something that was never dead
The blessing was successful, the Incubus never came back
But she always wondered if someone else was under attack!

Spell Bound

The seasoned wizard sits amongst his many books
His raven sits on the back of his chair, he watches and looks
He's reading a text to find the perfect spell
One that will send his enemy straight to hell

He was ancient when my grandfather was just a child
Living in a cottage in the old woods, wild
Legend has it he's the darkest wizard of all
The forest animals are constantly at his beck and call

His chalice filled with a steaming hot brew
All the while he's choosing which spell to pursue
It appeared that steaming chalice was a permanent fixture
Only the ancient wizard was aware of what's in his mixture

One of his favorite spells allowed the wizard to shape shift
Perhaps a mean old wolf that was guile and swift
Or a wizened owl that hunts his prey by night
He could gather information by staying out of sight

I, myself, would never want to be the wizard's enemy
Not with his cunning and intelligent personality
He could turn me into a tree stump with the blink of his eye
If I was no longer the princess, I think I would just die!

Spirit of Love

Lightning strikes in the background
Yet a rainbow can still be found
Do not think of it as a raging storm
Look within your heart, our spirit's form

When we trod the red road on Turtle Island
Our love shone like a sparkling diamond
Inseparable, whether day or night
Never wanting out of the other's sight

Then white man came, our lives' were changed
But we refused to let us become estranged
We were forced to walk, "The Trail of Tears"
There was no choice but to face our fears

Our woven blankets, riddled with disease
Tears shed by Great Spirit, no way to appease
His bravest children died at his feet
This white man's illness, you could not cheat

The option of survival had been taken away
We took to the heaven's the very same day
Look to the rainbow, high in the sky
Our spirit of love just will not die…

March

———◈❦◈———

March, home to warmth of change
Or, march on to further destruction
The wind, sounds of a battle cry roar
Reluctantly, winter departs
The beautiful crocus pokes through
Unsure if it wants to be seen
The changing of the guard
The equinox, season of the hawk
It is the metamorphic season
Snow turns to blood, sweat and tears
As the lion devours the sacrificial lamb...

The Journey

Hiding from the sun
Greeting the rain
Thunder obscures my sobs
Wind burns my face
As I walk this road
An arduous journey
I see you along the way
Your moccasins fit my feet
Certainly, we could trade
Though, nothing would change
The scenery appears different
Walking in circles
Wash, rinse, repeat
Faces are diverse
Each person is the same
There are no hero's today
To save me from me
And you from you
Time after time
The hero we seek
Is inside of us…

Real Men Cry

All my live I've heard, "Big boys don't cry"
For the life of me, I never understood why
I think it takes a real man to shed a tear
Born with emotions, why should he fear?

When saline rivers run down his rugged face
A man shouldn't worry, if his tears leave a trace
Whether tears of sorrow, or tears of joy
What does it matter, if he was born a boy?

The things men do, the things men see
Can be too much to cope with, apparently
With many complications, life can be grim
It's all one can manage, to sink or to swim

When a grown man cries, I want to hold him tight
Compassion rises from my heart, at very first sight
Because crying for a man is considered taboo
I wish to be there, and aide with his rescue

But, I know in my heart, he needs to let it out
Whether he just has tears, or he sobs and shouts
It's unhealthy to keep it in, even if you're a man
We were born with these emotions, I'm a big fan!

An Oyster and a Pearl

With you on the other side of this Earth
How can I explain just how much you're worth?
You know how to make my heart skip a beat
Whenever I read your words, I have to take a seat

Our connection may be hard to understand
But it's very real, the writing's in the sand
My belly get's uneasy, just like a school girl
It appears like we fit, like an oyster and a pearl

You have said that light shines from my heart
But, how can you see it, when we're so far apart?
When I search the night sky, stars refuse to shine
Once we're together, everything will be just fine

You claim you're my frog, and I your princess
I've never been royalty, this I must confess
You're my knight in armor, coming to my rescue
Certainly not a frog my dear, it's just not true

I'd like to enjoy this life, with you at my side
You're planted in my heart, I really must confide
The secret's out, the cat's out of the bag
Now we just need to live, under the same flag

Please don't hurt me, or break my heart in two
Tell me you feel the same, tell me it's true
I have no more heartbreaks, left inside of me
Sweetheart, please come, and cross the open sea!

People Care

We are Humans For World Peace
It does not take expertise
If everyone could live and let live
Offer their hand, and then give

I've been to world peace rallies before
People from all over the globe explore
Many nations gather for universal prayer
It's beautiful to see, all these people care

Why can't it be like that everyday?
It would be, if I could have my say
I see no purpose in fighting a war
No one ever wins, this is for sure

It takes too much energy to hate
Why can't we all just negotiate?
If people lived without greed
Be kind, and give to those in need

Earth would be a much better place
What does it matter about race?
Everyone's color is the same on the inside
It's time to be brother's and sister's with pride!

Sheila the Selkie

There's a tale from old Irish folklore
One very interesting, you may want to explore
Creatures called "Selkies" that live as seals
Also as women, the story reveals

Local men would steal the seal skin
Because the Selkie would have to stay women
Arthur aquired his beautiful wife this way
He and Sheila married by the sea one fine day

Arthur was a fisherman on the rough sea
Sheila stayed home, cared of the house beautifully
Selkies enjoy solitude, but make excellent wives too
The husbands enjoy everything the Selkies do

Sheila at times would miss being a seal
She'd go to the water to capture the feel
Her husband Arthur, didn't really understand
But he wanted Sheila happy, he did not demand

When a Selkies man was out to sea
They would sing by the harbor, endlessly
Thinking the boat was lured by their voice
Sheila sang for days, she had no choice

Arthur's boat never came home, he was lost
Sheila sang her heart out, at any cost
After some time, she wanted to be a seal once again
But with her skin gone, she had to stay a woman

Dorinda Wheeler

Never leave your attire out of sight
If it's stolen, you're in for a fight
Especially if you're a Selkie at the sea
That is the moral of this old story!

Dark Raven

Dark Raven was an Indian princess.
A beautiful woman, I must confess.
Like a frolicking fawn on a spring day,
She looks like her mother, I must say.

Searching for berries, a white man shot her.
It wasn't deadly, but caused quite a stir.
The burning shrapnel caught her right in the face.
Getting her to the medicine woman was a speedy race.

He hit her left cheek, it was almost gone.
The hunter didn't know, but was clearly wrong.
The medicine woman was sickened, ready to fight
Unsure if Dark Raven would lose her sight.

The problem being, it left a terrible scar.
You could see her malady from afar.
She could finally see it, from a reflection in the lake.
Horrified, she wished it was a terrible mistake.

It took some time, but eventually found who did this.
Dark Raven gathered some warriors, that would not miss.
They took after him, with bloodlust in their eyes.
Hopefully, they could catch him by surprise.

On their journey, a warrior became smitten with the princess.
He was young, handsome, and virile, I must confess.
His attention made her feel so much better.
She checked with her parents, so they could confer.

Her warrior thought she was beautiful as the brightest scar.
To him, Dark Raven was more lovely then any, near and far.
The wedding was planned for after the harvest this year.
The couple was in love, and happy, with nothing to fear…

Equinox

As the spring flowers blossom.
My heart has begun to wilt.
Like we are each a separate equinox,
or we are polar opposites.
The fresh breath of spring
comes whispering in.
At the same time, I feel like,
I'm decaying from the inside.
It's getting warmer with each passing day,
yet, I am chilled to the core.
My leaves have gone from hues,
of red, orange and gold, to brown,
dried up, and blowing away.
I'm on the verge of being a bare tree.
Those brown leaves are my soul.
I have given and given,
yet no one is there for me.
All used up, nothing but dust.
There's nothing left to do, but,
sweep me up, and toss me away.
While the rest of the world,
is coming out of hibernation.
I wish to sleep,
sleep,
sleep,
sleep,
until I never again wake.

Nobella Waits

Atop the old mountain range,
Nobella, the majestic matriarch,
watches over her terrain.
She's grand with her purple and blue hues.
Yet, she look's and is very menacing,
like a rattlesnake ready to strike,
or a cougar waiting to pounce.
The elves and the gnomes,
and also the fairies and the pixie's
reside below her mountain top perch.
They saw her wrath when her mate
took his very last breath. Devastated was she.
So, now everyone walks on shards of glass
hoping to never see her wrath again.
Still, Nobella sits and waits.
Her talons alone could rip your head off,
with a single swipe, and with a swish of her tail,
she can disembowel someone easily.
Then there's the fire Nobella exhales.
It can take out a village with a single breath.
Absolutely no one wants that to happen.
Before she took her point, her mate and she
flew over the valleys to reek havoc, but
those days are gone forever.
Still as a statue, Nobella waits with anticipation…

Day Dreams and Night Scenes

Night time is her domain.
The still darkness inundates her.
She is a nocturnal being,
just like her cat, her familiar.
Sleeping all day long.
Better yet, if it's raining.
The demons show their ugly faces,
when the sun comes up 'til dusk.
Her dreams come to her, as if
she's watching a black and white film.
As a child, the recurring dreams
came, and have yet to leave.
An evil being is in full chase,
as she walks past the bone yard.
She tries to run, but,
her legs become paralyzed,
like two heavy logs.
seconds before the entity
puts claws into her,
she awakens and is screaming.
Drenched to the bone.
Clammy from saline sweat.
Now and again, she will encounter
a really nice dream.
Hoping to never awake.
Just let it play through,
like on a reel to reel film.
Sleeping is her other realm,
where she is the queen.
If she has a lucid dream,
she's like a majestic owl,
who soars in silence to catch

his prey. Like the owl, she can
plan her direction and destination.
The world is his playground,
with his large, round, amber eyes.
At the witching hour, she is
harmless until provoked.
On the other hand, her familiar,
Gemini, guards her at all hours.
If you dare to enter their dominion,
it's at your own RISK!

Continue On

You were the most handsome man,
I've ever had the privilege to know.
You proved to me that chivalry is NOT dead.
Opening doors for me, so sweet.
Holding my coat as I try to get it on.
It felt more like a straight jacket
when I tried to do it myself.
You held my chair, as I was about to sit.
These are the things that I remember,
growing up as a little girl.
As an adult, I had a rude awakening.
I may stand for women's rights, but
I'm also into good manners, and
treating a lady as such. I learned
by example. My dad did those things.
Growing up, I guess I assumed...
But, now you're gone. Gone forever.
Speaking for only myself, you will
certainly be missed. You became ethereal,
like an angel, when you passed. I have
no doubt about this. You were heavenly
on earth, I'm sure they held a special
spot just for you. Not everyone
saw this side of you. To them, you were
quite depressed, stand-offish, maybe
even a bit rude. I saw through
all of that and found a flower
blooming in the desert. In a place
where flowers do not bloom.
I'm sorry for the people who never
took the chance to know the real you.
For they have missed so much...

So I lit a candle for you and for them.
They needed that candle more then you.
While sitting in the emergency room
with you, I saw a little smile and you
were gone. As soon as they said,
"time of death 9:37 pm, I witnessed a
flowing white mass heading for the
light over head. It validated the idea
of "going to the light". I was a witness.
Never have I had an inkling of where
you were headed. I cradled your
empty shell for awhile, just as a mom
swaddles her newborn. Going home
alone that night, was the loneliest
thing I have ever done. As I lit that
candle, it was for the ones left back
to continue on their miserable lives.
The ones that never saw the real side
of the beautiful person I knew...

Too Many

———·⟨⊰◈⊱⟩·———

So many tea lights lit in rows,
for each day I wait for you.
Even one is too many.
Like every time the police
have heard, "I've only had two"

My Breath

You can smell spring.
Glorious
like fresh baked cookies.
The lilacs are in bloom.
The aroma lingering,
making me feel like new love,
or even pixie's leaving
tiny little crystals on the grass.
It simply take's my breath away.

Had It All

Not only did this angel fall
but her feathers fell too
falling hard, like a snow squall
losing everything, what is she to do?
because sadly, she once had it all

Bide the Time

———— ❖ ————

Today, the fool steps into the abyss.
Going with blind faith, without knowing
what he's in for, or what he'll miss.
It's his time to go forth and start showing.

This will not be the demise of the fool.
There will be life lessons at every bend.
In his path, he will learn, but not from school.
Life isn't always kind, but it's not the end.

The first of April is designated to he.
Silly, practical jokes are done at his expense.
The fool tries to avoid it all desperately.
In the back of his mind, he keeps a reference.

Knowing the laws of karma, he bides his time.
Threefold, the pranksters get hit one by one.
His naivety is not his fault, nor his crime.
Expertise takes time, not quite so fun.

I envy the fool, as he can trust all things
It's the beginning of the dance, stepping on toes.
Still not jaded, he whistles and sings
The end of the dance is the beginning of woes.

False Courage

She is all grown up, mature
Her road has been rocky, uneasy
With little trust for anyone, she's sure
Reflecting over her past, she feels sleazy

The childhood she recalls was insane
With abuse of every kind, she made it
A resilient, troubled child, not to blame
Physical, emotional, mental, sexual, a composite

An introvert, she was so very shy
So withdrawn, "Don't speak 'til spoken to"
Treated so poorly, without knowing why
To "Be seen and not heard", it's true

Turning to drugs and alcohol at a tender age
It seemed to be the right thing at the time
Rebellious, with false courage at this stage
Repressed memories, she became sublime

Failed marriages, children, self medicate
It appeared in her delusion to keep demons at bay
She needed to sober up, it was her fate
But, the demons, ugly and powerful were at her each day

Memories were slipping in, one by one
Professional help, learning to cope and deal
Early on, it became worse, coming undone
It took time to understand, it was all real

A survivor, getting stronger and stronger with time
Yes, there are set backs, many triggers and such

Eventually realizing, her life had become a crime
Still, she craves affection, she is in need of touch

After many years, her inner child still needs healing
She may be all grown up, but partly still a child
With "perps" still alive, it's hard to grasp her feeling
She has survived, and she's no longer wild

Such a shame, her kids experienced such things
With many years sober, there's still work to do
A fresh canvas, she paints a child with wings
Representing her life and how she got through...

Legends of '69

Like wildfire, the word was spread
An army came for The Grateful Dead
Rainbows of blue jeans and of tie-dye
Clouds of flower-children getting high

The Catskills would never be the same
Woodstock Festival, their claim to fame
Janis and Jimi, so many more
Resonated through the valley floor

Legends were made in that field of dreams
The sky opened, pouring happy screams
Chants of sex, drugs and rock-n-roll
The world witnessed a weekend of soul

A distraction from the war at hand
The loss of many on foreign land
Lethal combat, not ours to fight
Boys became men in that fateful plight

I was but a child way back when
Observing it all on channel ten
Opinions were cast around my home
That summer hippies and soldiers roamed

Scrying

Gazing intently, a black bowl
Reflection of another soul
Divination, I question thee
The mirror echo's back at me

Clairvoyant, I'm able to see
Near future, divine prophecy
Or peer deeply, into the vast
Who was I in lives of the past?

Necromancer, or maybe witch
But my magic, is not pitch...

Forevermore

A Cajun girl from the bayou
Became a priestess of Voodoo
Seeking out immortality
She ended up a casualty
Eternal youth is what was sought
Though, misery is what she bought
All those she loved had passed away
Forevermore, she's here to stay...

Sweet Release

The glass slipper, not meant to fit
Pursuit of her prince, she'd not quit
Thought she'd found him, his trophy wife
Demon in guise, destroyed her life

Deficient dreams to her dismay
Stolen confidence, lost her way
Unfortunate, her mind's not free
A single mom, mother of three

Cherished children, her greatest wealth
But stress has compromised her health
Starting to age, starting to fade
Relinquishing pain with a blade

Sweet release while carving skin
Blood-letting evil, from within
Anguish eases, dripping of red
Mutilation, addiction fed

Abhorrent maps on the surface
A mask of lines serve no purpose
Beautiful woman, blinded eyes
Tragically, she does not realize...

Reminiscing

A man of valor, man of word
Guardian of game, fish and bird
His childhood dream, satisfied
Natures champion, classified

Impressive in that uniform
With badge and holster, quite a storm
Reputation always on line
The poachers target by design

I held you in such high esteem
Even as a rebellious teen
So proud to have you as my dad
Though time was nothing to be had

A virile man, you left this plain
Catastrophic, my heart was slain
It's your birthday, I miss you so
As my perpetual hero

Reminiscing of days gone by
Saline rivers never dry
My sorrow is forevermore
Contentment I can not explore

Do NOT express time heals all pain
It's just different, not the same
Feeling abandoned, so alone
After all these years, still I moan...

Heartbeats

With the strike
of a blade,
death drips
with each
her shallow
heartbeats...

Sticks and Stones

Reduced to tiny shards of glass
Blown to hell with a buckshot blast
May have been fragile yesterday
Abusive words have had their way

Sticks and stones have nothing on names
Forever out there, up in flames
Who the hell do you think you are?
It's okay to leave another scar?

Psychosis doesn't make you tough
Apologies are not enough
Deeper in the abyss I fall
No light, nor floor, not even wall

A little boy, not a real man
I must admit, I'm not a fan
Love you so much, my youngest one
You've burned that bridge, so now I'm done

Should you ever make your amends
Accepting of them will depend
No more names, no more disrespect
Hateful words have lasting effect

When I'm gone, do not dare shed a tear
It's way too late my darlin' dear
Do not take it out on your wife
All of that guilt carried for life...

Country Girl

Explore my body, soul and mind
Please try to explain what you find
My life, always a mystery
Nothing that will make history
I'm interesting just the same
There will be no fortune and fame
An easy going country girl
Living life on a tilt-a-whirl...

Searching (Triolet)

Snowy Owl away from home
Beautiful creature of the wing
Just a little south of your zone
Snowy Owl away from home
Searching for prey the fields you comb
Asking questions, you do not sing
Snowy Owl away from home
Beautiful creature of the wing

Temptation (Adult Content)

Images of you dance in my head
Young and virile, much to be said
Sensual body, does not quit
Rival in appeal is your wit

Not just your member, but your brain
Temptation is so hard to restrain
Sweep me away in fantasy
Forbidden knight brings ecstasy

Ravish my body, head to toe
Fill me up 'til I over flow
Pink petals, a perfect flower
Sweet nectar you must devour

Wet kisses 'til you're on fire
Fill me to depths of desire
United as one, drenched in sweat
Leave me with pearls, a matching set

Hurry, I'm melting into you
Though what we have might be taboo
I'm on the edge, living wild
Playing it safe, not my style

Though you're a man half my age
I'm nothing but a fleeting stage
Different if tables were turned
A double standard I have learned...

Daily Resolve

As the last grains of sand flow
Through the annual hour glass,
I reflect upon those I've adored
And those I have lost
No regrets, no mistakes
Only lessons learned
I have erred as all do
My flaws are many
Keeping them in check
A daily resolve...
As I rest my head
Upon the downy pillow
Pondering the day,
Did I do my best,
Or let it slip away?
Make changes where available?
Try to make a difference,
One granule at a time?
And when the opportunity
Arrives to bequeath,
For the dawn of a new year,
Love more, hate less
Take no hostages
Strive to be a better human being...

Scandalous

An evil entity
Her darkness all can see
Nefarious, her ways
Sinister tricks she plays
Debauched queen, salacious
Her ways are scandalous
A dark heart to core
Expected from a whore
Climb off the depraved poll
Save your infamous soul...

The Phoenix

Rising from hot ashes, the Phoenix
Flying high away from cynics
Warp speed, flames from his talon feet
The Challenger could not compete

Shaking the debris from his wings
Out of the dust, leaving smoke rings
The mighty beast can not be kept
In flight, free from bondage, he wept

Now an amazing bird of prey
Focused, no longer free to stray
Beautiful, proud as a peacock
Yet he never frequents a flock

Survival

I am of the First People
Living life to the fullest
Taking nothing more
Than we can use
Uninvited, they arrived
Full of want, of greed
Unkempt promises; lies
Thieves and murderers
Genocide; evil to the core
Land stolen, raped of pride
Cut our hair, steal our voice
We survive, despite you

Lost Sensations

Azure pools catch my glance
Your aura, warm, inviting
Aromatherapy, puts me at ease
Arousing lost sensations
Ships passing in the night
Now fully aware
My world, affected for eternity...

Reflections

Always running, never still
Force to be reckoned with
Deeper than one might know
Yet, you ride my back
Looking at me, seeing yourself
A mirror collage; reflections merge
I'm a cool customer
Allowing access to my world
Wet and wild...

Gone, Not Forgotten

Feeling your presence
Your fragrance I still smell
My dreams you visit
I shall always love
And never forget you
Though years continue
To pass...

Sacred Solstice

Dancing about on icy snow
The moon is full and all aglow
Kiss me under the mistletoe
Winter Solstice
The nights shorten, however slow
Crystal coldness

Drifting

Yesterday's breath
Lingers on my pillow
With haunting dreams
Visions of you
Continue on
Drifting away
Unable to return
Forever out of reach
A mere memory...

Hell Bent

Freaked out, just what was I to do?
Obviously not de ja vu
Doppelganger, a "shadow self"
Lose your life or at least your health

"Double Walker", not safe to see
Shape shifter, evil entity
Malevolent wraith, disappear
To see myself, can't help but fear

Lost in chaos, twisted brain
My tortured soul, alone with pain
Mental image, you broke my heart
Haunted memories, from the start

I am hell bent, a ruined life
Making me sick, causing me strife
Cataloged visions, branded mind
Terrorized, forever confined

Dance to beats of a silent drum
Misunderstood, where am I from?
The likeness of me took it's toll
Now on display in a fish bowl...

Spreading Joy

He's a ruby throat beauty
His wings on double duty
Spreading joy along the way
With Rose of Sharon everyday
Sipping nectar with his straw
Watch with wonder and with awe
He's a unique little guy
'Cause of the way he can fly...

Your Wicked Ways

Though shrouded in obscurity
Mind full of insecurity
Sunken deep into the abyss
Hoping for death's eternal kiss

Foul demons have taken your soul
Left with a heart blacker than coal
Possessed and obsessed, evil preys
Diabolical, sinister plays

So far from any kind of light
Indiscernible is your plight
Who could ever love this clouded heart?
All hope lost from the very start

Necromancy, a moonless night
Your wicked ways ready for flight
So nefarious to the core
It's time for God to declare war...

Contrast

The seasons first snow
Crisp, lies at my feet
Seems cold and harsh
As the the years of deceit

Bright white, such a contrast
A glare to my eyes
Like love you professed
And all of your lies

We loved like crazy
Fought just as hard
Then the ace of spades
Was your final card

Your last word rang clear
As you lay there dead
Time has been passing
With more to be said

I can't sleep at night
Without haunting dreams
Your beautiful face
I awake with screams

You, my Prince Charming
Locked in your castle
Many years of this
More than a hassle

I was your princess
Then your wedded wife
It faded away
A prisoners life

Still, fond memories
Invade all reason
Once 'twas magical
Now pain filled treason...

In Her Keep

Hades pet from the underworld
The Chimera becomes unfurled
From demonic legions she is formed
Animal features she has scorned

Beware the beast, she hungers meat
Raw and bloodied, you're at her feet
Before you chance to blink an eye
Without a moment to defy

You pray your God His mercy now
Yet it's to Hades you're forced to bow
Your worst nightmare has come to life
Silver Chimera was once your wife

Illusion or reality?

Deep within, it's your bride you see
Is it a possibility?
She is such a monstrosity

Somehow you try to make sense of this
Your body quakes from the abyss
Sharp talons wake you from your sleep
Vivid memories in her keep...

Four Seasons

It's a crisp, chilly Autumn day
Sun shines though I am feeling gray
Winter's arriving, I dismay
Keep snow at bay, keep snow at bay

Critters fill for seasonal rest
Adding many pounds is their quest
Blue Jays appear to squawk in jest
All done with zest, all done with zest

Winter appears before you know
Beautiful little flakes of snow
It's Mother Nature's finest show
The wind shall blow, the wind shall blow

Shoveling paths, no desire
The kid next door is for hire
Cocoa and a crackling fire
Lets retire, lets retire

Tiny crocus' pop through the snow
Colorful flowers really show
Blustery winds of March do blow
Winter must go, winter must go

Days grow longer, become so fair
As spring arrives without a care
Shedding the layers, almost bare
Foaling the mare, foaling the mare

Dorinda Wheeler

Skin sticking to the vinyl seat
Kids everywhere with grubby feet
Summer embraces us with heat
It can't be beat, it can't be beat...

Jealousy

The proverbial green eyed monster
Can't see straight with weeping eyes a blur
If you can't trust him then what's the use?
Seems to be a form of self-abuse
"But she's more beautiful and she's smarter
All of that and it's just for starters"
This tenacious beast will chase him away
Self-fulfilled prophecy, he WILL stray
Your heart may feel as if it'll burst
If he doesn't accept you at your worst
He doesn't deserve you at your best
Be confidant and know you are blessed....

Don't Send Flowers

Alone, she resides on the skirts of town
Agoraphobia keeps her home-bound
Visitors rare, children who don't care
Dwelling in a constant state of despair

Thelma to her Louise, her only friend
Countless hours they planned for the end
Once party girls, their spirits now broke
Popular then, now the brunt of a joke

The notion of dying leaves her in peace
Refusing to speak of her dis-ease
How long would the realization be?
Who would find her body eventually?

Common place to be unseen or unheard
Shed NO tears when you finally get word
Don't send flowers when you didn't before
Consumed with guilt, you should've loved her more

She only desired your company
Conversation, perhaps some empathy
You thought her crazy, all in her head
Don't you feel stupid, now that she's dead?

Forever Beautiful

Observing folks milling about their day
From my favorite haunt sipping Earl Gray
Inconspicuous, morphing out of sight
People watching long into the night

Programmed, just going through the motions
A grind, no individual notions
Productivity, watching bottom lines
Stifled artists losing their minds

Gauche, inept teenagers on a first date
Single moms, crazed, forever late
Clandestine meetings, cheating on the wife
Disabled Vets, hated for their life

No one signed up for this, long gone goals
Some contract Satan, promises of souls
They nerve to snivel come collection day
Stupid cowards, shut up and pay

From my peripheal vision, there's hope
An elderly couple who learned to cope
Hand in hand they happily stroll
Sixty years hasn't taken it's toll

Serious their vows, the good and the bad
No one bailed, made best of what they had
They have each other and that's enough
Grateful in life when you learn to hang tough

"He told me I was beautiful each day
Shines from within me in every way"
He's made her feel this way through the years
"My blushing bride" as he wiped the tears...

Hushed Tones

From richness of Autumn's grace
Colors and silhouettes embraced
Hearing melodic rapture
Seasonal tones are captured

Summer's harmony long past
Intermittent promises cast
Birth, death, rebirth; constant change
Plans made, often rearranged

Reflecting on days gone by
Golden leaves whisper and sigh
Listen closely with your heart
A cycle ends, another starts

Your devotions loud and clear
"I love you darlin'", in my ear
Hushed tones are in the air
Silence deafens without care...

Snow-Flake

From deep within the forest
A puma roars with might
On his breath, blusters in
The winters first storm
Snow and sleet tapping
Gently on the window panes
Of our one room cabin
Your musk, sweeter than
Hot cocoa steaming in mugs
Bodies entwined on the bear rug
Your kisses seer my skin
Like a brand on flesh
I tingle more with each caress
Your log in my fireplace
An avalanche of heat crackles
From your cherry wood
Sweat drips like sap
From maple trees
Desire runs ramped as
Snow piles up higher
Sheltered in your love
I couldn't feel safer
Our love is unique as each
Individual snow-flake . . .

Tried and True

I used to be young and pretty
Maybe even a bit witty
But times have changed and I have grown
Learn a lot living on your own

I've been married and now I'm not
But the lessons I've not forgot
There's a reason for everything
Many memories I can bring

Now I just age like real fine wine
Lusty bouquet and more refined
The wisdom I would never trade
Life is no longer a charade

Beauty fades, knowledge does not
I would never trade my spot
This place I earned, tried and true
Can't believe how much I grew...

Cabin Fever

It is the Autumn of my life
Clouds above turning gray
With winter quickly approaching
Soon the cold and the snow
Each day starving for life
Yet dying inside just a bit more
Limbs so brittle they break and fall
Shoveled into a nursing home
Angry children waiting for the inevitable
With melted hearts, streams run
Tears saturate and breathe new life
A grandchild born, buds blossom
"She has your mother's eyes"
All is bright and beautiful
After the spring showers
Brought about by their guilt
The summer of my children's lives
Green grass, flowers and fun
Harvest is quickly approaching
And they shall reap what they sow
Their beauty peaked now declining
Drying up and becoming barren
Gray clouds again mingle above
The cycle is repeating, depleting
Ashes to ashes, dust to dust
'Til one day they become a burden
To THEIR darlings
At last they feel the pain
The loneliness, the cabin fever
Of a long, hard winter, hungry for life
And alas, begging for death...

Red Flags

I see your breath upon the wind
Time to barricade, deep within
Dark shadows, they whisper my name
Disconnected, a bit insane

There's no change when nothing changes
Ignoring signs just deranges
Drowning in fear, no air above
Desperation to feel the love

Kaleidescope thoughts, twist some more
Prisms of light are at the core
Grasping at hope, still on the ledge
Reel me in, I'm over the edge

Voices screaming inside my head
Why don't I listen? Flags are red
Ephemeral sanity slips
Fleeting as a lunar eclipse

I see your breath upon the wind
Too vulnerable, must rescind
Stop the ride, my world's a dump
What's the point? Might as well jump...

Raising Dead

Spanish Moss hangs from Cyprus Trees
Putrid stench lingers on the breeze
Deep in the swamp, the old bayou
At the place they practice Voodoo

A chartreuse fiend and a blue moon
This night won't be forgotten soon
The New Orleans queen conjured this
Demonic face in creepy mist

From the haunted French Quarter
Skeletons rose from the water
Satanic specters fill the air
Leave her frightened, full of despair

Murder and mayhem that very night
Swamp fog and eerie green light
Sacrificial blood streams and pools
Vapor rises as the air cools

Paralyzed, her feet full of lead
The priestess chanted, raising dead
Finally awakens in her bed
Heinous memories in her head...

Unholy

Sultry, sexy the legend declares
An air of evil that lends a scare
Do not look directly in those eyes
Her haunting beauty will mesmerize

Lascivious creature of the night
Raising desire from a single bite
Orgasmic throws, it's a wild ride
Awaken to an undead bride

Fear gels when reality sets in
Gone the enchantress, sexy vision
Before you lies a monstrosity
She's a lamia, you have to flee

Devouring men, her power's lust
Pray to your god, for she's unjust
Unholy on All Hallow's Eve
Redeem your self, her spell relieve

A message to those men weak for flesh
Beware the seductress, don't enmesh
Satan's minion, so damned guile
She'll steal your soul with wanton style...

Suffer the Witch

Jack-O-Lanterns and ghouls set the scene
Annually, the night of Halloween
Festive costumes for the masquerade
'Til the sun rises, they all parade

In all her glory she does bask
Behind the beauty of her mask
Identity hidden, no one knows
She's the Hag from behind the groves

Toadstools, pumpkin seeds, and bat wings
Around the cauldron she steps and sings
Quarters drawn and her circle cast
Raising power to the Goddess Bast

The transformation has taken place
With a veil of beauty and of grace
Now she's ready for the Samhain Ball
Incognito, she'll fool them all

"Suffer the witch", they'll cry in vain
And no one will ever see her pain
Ignorance is what sets them apart
Intolerant, from the very start

The mask fades with early morning light
She was not alone for just one night
Time to go, no more festivity
Solitaire, the Crone was meant to be...

Real Mccoy

Sexy, flashy, dashing and daring
Hot babes will be stopping and staring
Legion of minions, real McCoy
I am the original "bad boy"

They say, "dance with the devil you know"
Not waltzing with a dingy scare-crow
Step with caution, I won't be so coy
I am the original "bad boy"

Dear beauty, please allow me this dance
You love the darkness, this is your chance
Seduction with macabre, a mere ploy
I am the original "bad boy"
Sexy, flashy, dashing and daring
I am the original "bad boy"

The Choice

One's too many, yet never enough
Slow suicide, living is tough
Drinking and drugging to end the pain
Saturated brain, going insane

Every days choice, live or die
Within your soul, the answers lie
Peel the layers, shed the mask
Exposing oneself, a brave task

Baby steps, there's only twelve
Chapter five is where to delve
The program works, people may not
Stay with the winners, claim your spot

Stupid slogans dance in your head
"One day at a time" is what was said
Think it through before you use
You're aware, it's just an excuse

Does your bottom hide a trap door?
Frightful to think what's left in store
Thank you so for keeping it real
Made a choice, no longer my deal...

Changes

Another season about to turn
Reflecting on lessons learned
Motivated by passion and pain
Turning pages, I can't remain

Saline rivers I no longer cry
Riding the wind, my tears dry
Cleanse the soul, breathe new air
Rid old burdens, it's only fair

I have been burned black as coal
Strength emits from a tortured soul
Heal this heart, rip it from my sleeve
From deep within, I must believe

There was a time I gave it away
The price costly, but willing to pay
Maybe I'll walk forever alone
But, refuse to have a heart of stone

Never again, not just a wife
It's a new chapter, a new life
Motivated by passion and pain
Turning pages, I can't remain...

Golden Eagle

In cottony clouds, edge of peak
Above all else, you circle and soar
On thermal zephyr, your nest you seek
In sky above, the Earth's floor

The queen of the tallest tower
Alluring vision transcends all time
Gazing down on the smallest flower
A retreat in which borders sublime

This pallet stuffed with the finest down
YOU MADE YOUR BED, LAY IN IT
Ever so soft and fluffy, yet sound
Perfect in every way you befit

Golden Eagle, a majestic sight
With scrutiny, you find your prey
Stunning aerobatics, is your flight
Returning to roost by end of day...

Light Worker

Baby's are born every day
Perfect beings in every way
With age they can become polluted
Often brainwashed and convoluted

Those who roam in source of all light
Darkness rolls off, fight the good fight
Their aura shines with brilliant hues
Negative energy, they so refuse

Living life a breath at a time
Knowing each is equally sublime
Giving of themselves, paying forward
A smiling face, that's their reward

Not a person, a Human being
Never blinded, always seeing
Knowing that "being" is an action
An order in the highest of faction

A group, yet so often alone
Light Workers move to a diverse tone
Higher awareness to conscious mind
Moving ahead, never behind

Human being I strive to be
Love and light is the path for me
Knowing life can be surreal
Earth harmony, my ideal...

Coyote

Disheartened by the dawn of day
With a heavy heart, I still lay
Coyote's in sheep's clothing, cute and coy
Single out the wounded, that's their ploy

Shattered mirrors, prisms of my life
Too much sorrow, endless strife
Cruelness of today's society
Casting opaque veils over me

Suffer in silence, who's to care?
Life of solitude, such despair
Inner demons relish my soul
When the night turns black as coal

Wizened ancestors guide me through
Others spit me out before they chew
Coyote's waiting at every turn
Life lessons repeated, 'til I learn

Walk the red road, discard the lies
Shake the filth off I so despise
I'm the one who holds the power
You're the one they'll devour...

Notions and Potions

An alchemist with wild notions
Tossing about "magic" potions
Perceiving riches would soon unfold
By transforming metal into gold

Endlessly, she worked with a fury
Longing for pelf, there was a hurry
Around the clock in that dismal lab
Even in the dark, she'd take a stab

Becoming obsessed, her life a void
Temper short, she became annoyed
No wheeling back, she was in too deep
Beakers and test tubes lay in a heap

Insanity has taken control
Time invested, yet still no gold
Psychosis became her only friend
Sticking by her 'til the bitter end

Eventually found by rancid stench
The alchemist was a filthy wench
Standing on end, her unruly hair
Appearing deranged, an empty stare

Living in squalor, hoping for wealth
Evaporating her mental health
At the asylum she now resides
"I can make gold", she often confides...

Home

As I listen to trickling rain
It takes me to a place in my brain
Where the longhouse is where I call home
Covert where Mother's creatures still roam

Prior to the settler's coming for their claim
Stripping our pride, and causing shame
Creator gave us sweet serentity
Always sure of my identity

I was considered a woman wise
Not an embarrassment in their eyes
But admired with true revere
Before knowing this word called "fear"

Plethora of family in one house
Enjoying a meal of hunted grouse
A simple life that we once lived
Everyone had much love to give

Our purple mountains majesty
The forest was a tapestry
A simpler time on Mother's land
United we would always stand...

Blinded by Love...

Your love lit up
My starving heart
A beacon of trust
From the start

Your aura so bright,
Blind could see
Sun and moon hid
From shame of thee

Sunglasses to protect
My eyes
Blinded by love
I realize...

Chiron (Dark Terzanelle)

Uncanny beast, half man, half horse
Mythical and between two realms
Centaur's stampede with mighty force

Archery known to overwhelm
Associated with the rain
Mythical and between two realms

Not only strong, but has a brain
Known for slaying the demon, Mot
Associated with the rain

Mortal enemy of the drought
Chiron, brute of another time
Known for slaying the demon, Mot

With his bow, mighty arrows climb
Also known as the bull slayer
Chiron, brute of another time

Also known as for slaying of bulls
Like a train wreck, he's an eyeful
Uncanny beast, half man, half horse
Centaur's stampede with mighty force...

Raging Storm

Rolling thunder pounds way up high
Lightning dances from ground to sky
A raging storm intensifies

My senses heightened, out of pace
Heart quickening, can't help but race
From head to toe my fingers trace

Gazing intently into your soul
With eyes burning like blazing coal
Heated desire takes its toll

You slip inside, slowly at first
Rising temperature, about to burst
Before too long we quench our thirst

Bodies drenched with sticky sweat
Raging storm continues to threat
Falling asleep on sheets so wet....

Reaper, Angel of Death

He's the one, the angel of death
Just the same as the Grim Reaper
Coming to collect your dying soul
He has no pity, nor mercy or shame
It's his job, and he does it very well
He's the one, the angel of death
Given a roster, it must be completed
His list is done to absolute perfection
Coming to collect your dying soul
Every "t" crossed, and every "i" dotted
No doubt, he's a master of his trade
He's the one, the angel of death
A mere skeleton underneath his robe
What his scythe is for, I do not know
Coming to collect your dying soul
A monster that nobody wants to see
You can run, but you can't hide
He's the one, the angel of death
Coming to collect your dying soul...

Renovating

About one hundred, fifty years past,
tragedy struck, a three year old girl was killed,
at the hands of her father, 'twas aghast.
No one ever knew why her blood was spilled.

There was speculation, but the truth was never told.
Lily was so sweet, full of spunk and energy.
Such a lass, you wanted to hold.
The townsmen shocked, it could not be.

After all these years, the house stood empty.
For some reason, it just would not sell.
With so many rumor's, potential buyers let it be.
I suppose the people thought the house had stories to tell.

Eventually, a couple wanted to turn it into an Inn.
They were able to see the beauty of long ago.
It took a lot of scratch just to begin.
The money it took to complete, they didn't know.

A short time later, after the beginning of renovation,
strange things began to happen in the ole' house.
Things would move with no explanation.
They certainly weren't moved by a mouse.

The couple had heard of this kind of thing before.
So, they started asking questions all around town.
They were told all kinds of old folklore.
The stories they heard, left them with a frown.

After things kept, accidents and the like.
Eventually, they saw the spirit of a wee lass.

She had pretty hair, between two and four, just a tyke.
But after awhile, they saw a large black mass.

Not knowing what it was, they were scared as hell.
The house almost complete, they'd lose a lot of money.
The fight was over, and they rang the last bell.
Once again, the house stood empty…

The Boneyard

It was an ominous morning
with an opaque veil of mist
suspended over the bone yard.
Drifting through the lanes,
it felt as if eyes were on me
from every direction. Ancient
pines stood, nesting vultures,
akin to the Griffin. With never
ending vigilance, they are
guardians of the dead.

Haunting marble angels,
cherubs, and crosses, I was
in anguish. Too much sand
had passed through life's
hourglass. Family tombs
predated the Civil War, but
I couldn't find who I was
looking for.

The obscure weather fit my
mood, but I continued until
stumbling upon a peculiar
grave. Etched into the stone
was my name, date of birth,
and date of death; yesterday.
A chill ran up my spine like
a huge spider. How could
this be?
I wanted to be cremated!

The Birdcage

It's a very murky night,
almost bereft of light.
The repulsive, ogre of a man,
has her locked away
in an enormous birdcage,
made from ornamental
wrought iron.
It may be pretty, yet it's still
horrific to her.
She is steadfast, alone
and frightened, outside
in the dark.

Her imagination runs wild,
like horses on the range,
galloping, and kicking up dust,
as she thinks of what
he might do with her.
The stench of fear
permeates the air, like
fresh lilacs on a spring day.
In a panic, she thinks of escape.

The monster of a man, grabbed
her off the street she was working.
Thinking of how beautiful she is,
he kept the street-walker for a "pet".
Taking her from the birdcage
only long enough to paw, or to
perform "tricks" for him.
He's a falcon, she's a mouse.

Escape attempts have failed.
Until the last time, she was a success.
A permanent success, as she crossed
over, to the other side.

Nightmares Do Come True

Deep shadows amongst dark and light.
Forces of mayhem course your mind.
Pressure of peer's, the path appeared
benevolent, perhaps rebellious at most,
adding thrill to your young life.
Sand rushed the hourglass and your path
started to bend and curve, eventually,
becoming a maze. Less light and growing
darker by the year.

Lucifer's trickery at play. His minion's
guised as "friends". You followed them
into the first level's of hell, without question.
Iron bars and tragedy, no deterrent. "Fun"
was still to be had. Forces so powerful,
you lost your way, deeper into darkness.

The demons became more cunning.
Ingesting his golden elixir continuously,
suffering, reeling with internal anguish,
your mind twisted like a pretzel.
Warping cells, turning them to mush,
Lucifer really had you in his clutches,
like a rabbit in the talon's of an owl.
Hap-hazard attempts to find a source
of light, eluded with trickery, you gave up.

Madness whispered in your ears.
Subliminal messages around each bend.
The maze, more and more intense.
No colors left in the kaleidoscope
of your brain. Darkness lurked

and consumed you. He showed you
"candy" in my medication bottles.
With your lack of control, temptation
became too much.

The committee in your head never took a break.
Lucifer, the puppeteer, held tightly
to your strings. Not enough elixir or candy
to make it all stop, until finally,
the strings went slack. The game over,
he claimed his prize. Your lifeless face,
and discarded, empty shell is all I see.
My nightmare, now reality.
A worm, strategically placed
into my brain, by Lucifer, himself.

Soul Collector

I am not your god,
nor am I your devil.
They can't stop me,
only prolong the
inevitable.
For I am Death,
the soul collector.

I shadow your
every move.
In the end, when
the last granules
of sand hit bottom
of life's hourglass,
I am there to
harvest
you.

In Memory of...

———·❖·———

All the men and women,
who liberally gave time
and body, for our rights
and for our freedom.
Recognition has been
diminutive, inappreciable,
and at times, non-existent,
considering your brave
accomplishments.

You've guarded our rights,
our borders, the constitution,
and all amendments.
Giving us freedom of speech,
and the ability to put my pen
to paper.
I say, "Thank you!", to each
one of you. On this day and
every day, you are remembered!

I also remember my late parents.
They gave and worried endlessly,
to assure my life was better
then theirs.
Instilling good morals, good
values, along with manners,
so I'd grow up to be an
honorable, gracious, generous,
human being.

Today, I'm all those things,
thanks to my loving parents.

I miss and I love you both.
On this day, and every day,
you are remembered!

The Family Glue

Cancer, diabetes, heart disease,
you battled them all.
The strongest woman
I've ever known.
My mom.

Mom, you were always there,
tried to show how much you care.
We often didn't see eye to eye,
our relationship would intensify.

You taught me right from wrong,
and by example, how to be strong.
A true exemplar of integrity.
Nothing less then sincerity.

You were a survivor right from start,
and perservered a heavy heart.
It molded the woman you became.
Life was serious, not a game.

As your daughter, I'm very proud.
If only I conveyed it to you aloud.
I pray you understand how I feel.
My love for you I will not repeal.

Mom, I miss you so damned much!
If only I could feel your gentle touch.
You were always the family glue.
How you did it, I have no clue.

You made sure we never went without.
To your family, you were devout.
Never goodbye, but see you again.
Wish I knew exactly when...

The Crypt

---◆◈◆---

At the crypt, she remains.
The fallen angel with bloody stains.
Now alone at the cemetery,
she lingers for another quarry.

Her spoil left to decay,
cadavers pile up day to day.
Decomposing into bone,
close to a certain stone.

It's the tomb of her deceased lover.
He's a vamp, like none other.

Lucifer, Fallen Angel

Please, my pretty, join me in Hell.
Look me in the eyes, feel my spell.
Your soul be damned, you have no chance.
I've wanted you from the first glance.

I am an angel fallen from grace.
It's the darkness that I embrace.
I get off on evil and the macabre,
watching the damned plea and sob.

My name is Lucifer, if you please.
Satan himself, is whom I appease.
You held a seance, and summoned me.
Soon you'll be added to a necrology.

You should be careful with necromancy.
When I call for you, don't cry or plea.
You must remember, nothing's for free.
I'll show up when you least expect me.

You've made a choice, what's done is done.
Your soul is mine, and it'll really be fun,
as you incinerate 'til the end of time.
For me, it'll be extensively sublime...

Nip It In the Bud

When he wants to control you,
the people you see, things you do,
and it increases from day to day,
stop it while you can, without any delay.

He'll find hurtful names to call you.
It's verbal abuse, you know this is true.
Give yourself some extra credit.
Nip it in the bud, you need to stop it.

These are early warning signs.
Don't give in to his designs.
Abuse of any type will progress,
yet, his love, he will openly profess.

"I'm sorry Babe. It won't happen again.
I get so jealous, when you talk to other men".
"I can't live without you, please forgive me".
"You know I love you", all on bended knee.

Next time you'll surely get smacked around.
I hope you'll be alive, when you're finally found.
Abuse is like a tan, it gets darker over time.
Involve the police, it's a very gruesome crime.

All the signs of abuse, are written on the wall.
When you get that eerie feeling, don't bother to stall.
Keep a bag of clothes and some money, hidden in the car.
Before it escalates the next time, get away, and go very far!

Your Love

Candles casting a warm, sensual glow,
wrapping us up in velvety shadow.
The ambiance is all about romance.
Our bodies mold, as we begin to dance.

With Barry White's voice in the air,
you glide me across the floor with care.
Caressing me with your finger tips,
you express your love on tender lips.

My rose petals of pink, moisten like dew.
The temperature rises as I respond to you.
Moving in rhythm, my heart skips a beat.
I know it's because of our body's heat.

My back to the wall, I feel your love.
You fit inside me like a silky glove.
We sway along with the stereo.
It may be dancing, but not the Tango.

Too Many…

My tears,
there have been many.
Saline creeks,
run from face to bosom.
Too many,
I have loved and lost.
For all eternity,
in a short stretch of time.
People say,
"time heals all wounds".
Not true,
no amount of time heals.
These wounds,
shroud me in darkness.
Blanket me,
like a lunar eclipse.
Nocturnal forces,
an owl on the hunt.
No escape,
the loneliness envelopes me.
These demons,
my only companions.

First Date

My searing heart quickens, as I await.
Today is to be, our very first date.
Anxious butterfly's dance in my core.
Like a nervous rabbit, out to explore.

Will I meet expectations, placed on me?
I wonder to myself, full of curiosity.
Insecurity floods the gate to the dam.
Rushing over me, the woman I am.

Can't help wonder, if there's chemistry.
Or will our flaws, show up tremendously?
Without a spark, there can be no flame.
I hope we ignite each other, just the same.

Will he kiss me, or will he make me wait,
until we go out again, on another date?
Patience has never been my best virtue.
I wonder, will we both want to pursue?

Time Between Time

Magical, mystical, hours of twilight.
Just before morning, just before night.
It transcends a time between time.
Expect the unexpected, so sublime.

Where Fae Folk dance, and Pegasus fly's.
Mythical creatures like dragon's arise.
Firefly's and Peepers, when it's warm.
Spirits in fog begin to form.

Peepers serenade, with an eerie song.
But, in twilight hours, nothing's wrong.
As the air cools, specters dance.
Risen from the grave, happenstance.

It's the time when dew will appear.
Alchemistic moisture, not to fear.
Obtuse vapors rise from the ground.
Necromancer's can be found.

Twilight's the perfect time of night.
So many oddities can come to sight.
Expect the unexpected, the only rule.
You may think me strange, but I'm no fool!

Unaware

Blissfully asleep on her bed.
Unaware of what's by her head.
A demon at the window leers.
Without knowledge, she has no fears.

The little dog wakes with a fright.
Shaking like a leaf, at the sight.
It utters a menacing growl,
at the evil spirit, so foul.

The entity is there for the child.
One move and the pooch goes wild.
While sugar plums dance in her head,
the dog keeps away the dead.

The Essence of You...

Friday, the first time I gazed
my emerald eyes upon you,
your distant radiant smile lit
up the cold, dank space my
heart once resided.
I felt the freedom of bondage
in the vast abyss of my soul.
No longer was I a prisoner
of distant pain and delusion.
Hundred's of horrific memories
were erased as easily as chalk
on a blackboard, and no longer
tattooed upon my brain.
Is it safe, I wondered, to step
into the sunlight of your azure
eyes?
Eyes that danced, and shined
so brightly upon me...
My body awakened with the
brilliance of a bon-fire on a dark,
starless eve.
My precious, pink rosebud
twinged with delight for the first
time in a thousand days or more.
My body now alive with desire
for you, for your touch...
For you are a true mercenary
of love.
Once starved for affection, now
fulfilled with the essence of you...

For All Eternity

We met one ominous, eerie night.
No Milky-Way gems or Luna in sight.
One glance, and you fell promptly in love.
Thought I was a gift, from heaven above.

Gazing at you, I immediately thought,
"Now this is the one, I have eternally sought".
I could get lost in your blue, cobalt eyes.
The deep ache of loneliness, now subsides.

Chatting for hours, talking about forever.
You were to embark on such an endeavor.
No way of knowing, no way to tell.
You were completely, under my spell.

Blinded by love, you never really knew.
A deer in the headlights, you had no clue.
We did not meet by happenstance.
You were chosen, under circumstance.

All your emotions and memories, came in a flood.
After one bite, and your crimson, river blood.
Now you're an Undead, for all eternity.
You'll roam forever, as a monster like me!

Tethered

Saline droplets rise
as the tide of the sea.
Spilling forth like a spring
waterfall, melting away
the iciness of my tattered,
torn heart...
Though my emerald eyes
are full to the brim,
they see clearly for the first time.
They do not weep for you alone,
but, for other's, past and future.
As this soul is tethered to pain,
and to loneliness, it shall be
the only forever in my world.
But, now that you are gone,
and in a better place,
maybe there is hope for me.
Though your ghost is everywhere,
you are no longer tangible.
Just maybe, one day in the future,
there will be someone who is
deserving of me,
my love...

Tapes of Yesterday

The old asylum upon the hill,
may be closed, but, it's not still.
In its day, merely a dumping ground,
for the destitute and mentally unsound.

Chambers filled with strange contraptions.
Devices used to control a person's actions.
Torture guised as safe, sound therapy,
but, took away all their individuality.

Animalistic noises still resonate.
No means to appease or to compensate.
Echoes of suffering and of the insane.
Locked doors of sills and window pain.

Reliving their private hell in every way.
If they talked, they'd have no say.
Hit fast-forward, and then press play,
all the rewound tapes of yesterday.

Now empty, desolate rooms and halls.
Still you can hear tortured voices call.
Patients and staff should be long gone,
but, memories and specter's do live on…

Mesmerized

You call yourself, a "Skinny Lizard".
I feel magic, and see a wizard.
So enraptured by your spell,
mesmerized, you make me melt.

Out of my element, my comfort zone,
to hear your voice, on the telephone.
Dying inside, to hold you tight,
to feel your touch, seems so right.

You leave me wanting to let you in.
Dreaming of life with you, to begin.
It's the truth, I must confide,
what I feel, is bona fide.

I've admired you from afar.
You shine a light, like a star.
I imagine your tender touch.
Have I revealed, way too much?

Separated by many a mile.
I won't beg, it's not my style.
Adventure out, take a chance.
We could live by happenstance!

A Blizzard

Watching you dance with your demons,
makes my heart heavy,
like snow covered branches.
It breaks from the strongest winds
of a blizzard, as it blusters
and drifts the snow higher.
Put that needle away,
not in your arm.
Poison courses through your veins,
as if driving on black ice.
I watch with horror,
as you lose control,
and head directly for the trees.
My sorrow is more powerful
then a blizzard
with gale force winds,
and snow falling
at an alarming rate,
with no end in sight.
Sleepless nights,
I await the phone call.
Wondering, is this the night
you take your last breath,
as if it's the last flake to fall?
My pain from your addiction,
deep as the deepest snow bank,
will not melt until you are free…

After Midnight

Camping on Tombstone Hill,
after midnight,
spirits do instill.

Shadows dance
everywhere.
All I can do,
is stop and stare.

Disembodied voices,
in the dark.
Up my spine,
chills are stark.

Crimson eyes
glare down on me.
Is it an evil
entity?

Never have I seen
the likes of this.
Demons
really do exist.

Satan is known
to cajole.
By twilight hour,
he may possess my soul.

Malignity prowls
and gives a warning.
Will I live
'til the morning?

A Real Woman

Fluffy, white, summer clouds,
set adrift in azure skies.
I am cottony and soft,
pleasing to the eyes.

My curves wrap around,
like a big, warm hug.
Some think I'm heavy,
to this, I just shrug.

I'm so tired
of the 'zines,
sayin' skinny
is the scene.

I have a full,
ample bosom.
I'm nothing shy
of a real woman.

Plush and full
like a feather pillow.
Not thin and wispy,
like a Weeping Willow.

I'm sexy and sensual.
Passionate, not obscene.
Put together like a goddess,
and built jus
like a queen.

Prince Charming

Marshy ways,
lily pad days.
thoughts of you,
I shall pursue.
Just one kiss,
will be bliss.
Love,
Prince Charming

Da Ja Vu

Lying in the shallows,
with the stillness of death.
My sister was found,
stealing her last breath.

It had been so long ago,
but to me, it's still raw.
I can still hear the crows,
agitated, and yelling, "caw".

Sleepless nights, a plenty,
praying the phone didn't ring.
This time, it's my child,
doing the same, damned thing.

De ja vu, all over again,
results will be the same.
There are no winners,
in this deadly game.

Mother's Inn

Norman's mother owns the inn.
He kills her off and wears her skin,
then he personifies Mother.
A haunted place like none other.

Demonic spirits roam the halls.
Room eleven beckons and calls.
Death comes to all and their brother.
A haunted place like none other.

Veiled in black but for swollen eyes.
Norman's possessed and in disguise.
Veiled in black just like his mother.
A haunted place like none other.

Norman's mother owns the inn.
A haunted place like none other.

Little Miss Brass

Little Miss Brass,
sat on her ass,
watching tv all night.
Along came a ghost,
a demonic host,
causing a hell of a fright,
sending her screaming,
because she wasn't dreaming.
It was a funny sight!

Hell-Bound

Once alive but now I'm dead.
He didn't care for things I said.
Evil forces took over me.
Satan's minions apparently.
Now hell-bound for eternity.

I had enough of his abuse.
Things he did, there was no excuse.
Evil forces took over me.
Satan's minions apparently.
Now hell-bound for eternity.

I had to kill him, then myself.
No longer was I on that shelf.
Evil forces took over me.
Satan's minions apparently.
Now hell-bound for eternity.

The Chase

Late night by the cemetery,
something is quickly chasing me.
I've had this nightmare many years.
It has brought out my darkest fears.
Inside my brain it burns and sears.

I run and run until I sweat.
I'm so afraid, I won't forget.
I've had this nightmare many years.
It has brought out my darkest fears.
Inside my brain it burns and sears.

I always awake just in time,
before it commits mortal crime.
I've had this nightmare many years.
It has brought out my darkest fears.
Inside my brain it burns and sears.

Shine the Light

Enough darkness, no more shadows.
Time has come to open windows.
Open up the doors of my mind,
and leave the darkness well behind.
Shine the light, I'm no longer blind.

The time has come finally.
You don't have power over me.
Open up the doors of my mind,
and leave the darkness well behind.
Shine the light, I'm no longer blind.

Say goodbye, time for me to go.
You really packed a nasty blow.
Open up the doors of my mind,
and leave the darkness well behind.
Shine the light, I'm no longer blind.

Life was Simple

We hung out with friends smoking pot,
at the school, in the parking lot.
Way back when, in the good old days.
Life was simple in many ways.
So much more then old cliche's...

Jimi Hendrix and The Greatful Dead
The Woodstock Movement was widespread.
Way back when, in the good old days.
Life was simple in many ways.
So much more then old cliche's...

Draft cards were gone in history.
Civil rights, a time to be free.
Way back when, in the good old days.
Life was simple in many ways.
So much more then old cliche's...

My Heart

I've loved you for so many years.
We traversed numerous frontiers.
Yet still, I wept rivers of tears.
Though you're gone, my love coheres.

You were the love of my life.
Happily, you made me your wife.
My heart aches for you, it appears.
Though you're gone, my love coheres.

Without you, I am very lost.
I'd be with you at any cost.
Your death, catastrophic, it sears.
Though you're gone, my love coheres.

I've loved you for so many years.
Though you're gone, my love coheres.

Rebirth

I climb the sacred mountain
to find the cave,
the belly of the beast.
Dark and wet like mother's womb,
time has come to be reborn.
Naked and cold
in the deep, dank, dark cave.
No sleep for the whole time,
yet I dream after smoking
from the sacred pipe.
Hawk comes with a message
from Wakan Takan.
I do not understand.
Soon, spider comes.
Spider created first
written language
by spinning her web.
What does this mean?
I feel spider's crawling,
all over my body.
Because I still do not understand,
Bear, our sacred brother,
shows up to teach me
of hibernation, what it means
to return to the womb.
I dream and meditate.
Many grandfather's come to me.
I still do not understand
until I get back to the village.
The record keeper lies
on her death bed...

Shape-Shifter

She will appear
as all woman,
but is really
a wily daemon.
A creature of
in between time.
The hours of twilight
and dawn are prime.
A shape-shifter,
an alluring fox.
Brings you to tears
with her squeezebox.
Cunning and coy,
she's so erotic.
A real beauty,
very exotic.
She'll have you
under her spell.
How far you go,
only time will tell.
Just one look
into her eyes,
then it will be,
your demise.
It's impossible
to get away.
For your soul,
you'd better pray!

Captivated

Your smile lights up
the darkest sky.
A gorgeous beacon
from way up high.
Your eyes, that of
an azure lagoon,
when cast upon me
I begin to swoon.
Erotic shivers
go up my spine.
Tantalizing tingles
feel just fine.
You appeal
to my raw desire.
My loins aglow,
feeling on fire.
I'm captivated,
under your spell.
Ravish me, release me,
from my hell.
Our love
is serendipity.
Cupid's work?
A possibility.
Two souls together,
meant to be one.
We rock heaven, earth
and the sun.
The rhythm of our hearts
coincide.
Please, spend eternity
at my side!

The Faery's Realm

Beautiful and alive,
they tower.
An entire sea
of the Sunflower.
The sunflower's stretch
way up high,
trying to reach the sunshine
and sky.
In the breeze, they dance
on gentle wave.
Wee fae-folk roam
in their enclave.
They're always welcome
in this realm.
Unlike crows who pick
and overwhelm.
The faery's realm
is in between.
On the edge is where
they can be seen.
Where flowers meet grass
is where they guard.
On the outer edge
of you're yard.
Together the flowers
and faerys dance.
Existing in a world
of romance.
If you're lucky,
you'll see their face.
Best be quick
or it'll be trace.

Abracadabra

I mourn this death
like any other.
You, my sister
from another mother.
Words a plenty
I can never undo,
my razor tongue
really cut you.
Storms we've trekked
hand in hand.
I could always trust
you'd understand.
Yearning for the friendship
we once had.
Looking back, I feel
so very sad.
Reading my cards
looking for a sign.
I seek out the animals
hoping all will be fine.
My sincere apologies
I offer you.
Please forgive me,
my words ring true.
If by magic I could
cast a spell,
abracadabra,
all is well!

Within

So much fear and so much passion.
Yet, he knows he must take action.
Casting a circle made of fire.
He's a priest, she's a vampire.

Invoke his God, this holy one,
the Father, Spirit and the Son.
Frightened by waves of desire.
He's a priest, she's a vampire.

She tests his faith but doesn't win.
His God is there; inside, within.
Safe in his holy empire.
He's a priest, she's a vampire.

So much fear, and so much passion.
He's a priest, she's a vampire.

Truth

Way back when,
a moment in time.
You were young,
and life sublime.
Rose tinted glasses
covered your eyes.
Truth be told,
and no one denies.
Circumstance change,
times not your friend.
Truth is, all good things,
come to end.
Thought provoking,
need for resolve.
No change, no change,
one must evolve.
It's important
to talk your talk.
Even more so
to walk your walk.
Your personal truth,
is then told.
People will listen,
then behold.

Angel In the Light

You are so pretty,
angel in the light.
They say you died,
but I see you each night.
Salty streams are running
down Daddy's face.
Tells me no on can
ever take your place,
that you'll live
forever in our heart,
and how you loved me
from the very start.
"I tell him Mommy,
you are over there."
So pretty in the light
and clothes you wear.
"Why can't he see you Mommy,
just like me?"
"Daughter, I'm a spirit now,
body free.
I know that one day,
you will understand.
I'm sorry Daughter,
this was never planned.
Give Daddy a kiss,
I love him so much!
Tell him I said,
I will be in touch."
I still see her,
every single night.
She's so pretty,
an angel in the light...

On Tour

Who's the dummy here, me or you?
You really don't have a damned clue.
I'm possessed by a nasty demon.
Just wait, tonight you'll be screamin'!

I'll reach my hand into your back.
Your entrails, a delightful snack.
Just moments before you're dead,
I'll climb right into your head.

Then, off we go on a killing spree.
Now with a human host, I'm free.
The dummy was okay for awhile.
Honestly, not really my style.

Tonight when we go out on stage,
trust me, we'll be all the rage.
The audience won't expect a thing.
At least until the terror we bring.

By then, I'll need a new host.
Your body will be like burnt toast.
Ventriloquist and dummy no more.
This demon must go out on tour!

I can't stay with one for too long.
That is, if I want to stay strong.
I must possess another human host.
Otherwise, I'll become a mere ghost.

The Ancestors

It was a stormy Halloween night,
and the town was without power.
People were becoming more alarmed
with each and every passing hour.

No trick or treaters out this evening.
Not a single person on the street.
Terrified parents kept their kids in.
In fear of who or what they might meet.

Not a star in the sky, only clouds.
It was as dark as the blackest abyss.
Town folk were afraid of their ancestors
returning to seal a deadly kiss.

Tonight the veil is lifted for them
so they may enter this realm once more.
The ambiance so dark and dismal.
Everyone's frightened to the core.

Candle light flickered all over town.
The glow was pretty, but eerie too.
It made the Shadow People look freaky,
as they showed up out of the blue.

No body woke the next morning.
Everyone was killed in their sleep.
The ancestor's spirits were pure evil.
The townsfolk souls they came to reap.

Tainted Memories

Distant memories of the past
Apparitions of long ago
Players from a sinister cast
Nightmares I prefer weren't so

Apparitions of long ago
Haunt my mind with no remorse
I only wish it wasn't so
Tainted memories, sinful source

Players from a sinister cast
Torture my soul from days gone by
Evil poisons from wide and vast
I wasn't willing, did not comply

Nightmares I prefer weren't so
Infiltrating dreams 'til this day
Heinous laughter, I hear them crow
All I want is to run away

Winds of Change

She beckons to us on the winds of change
Autumn's alluring hues cover a wide range
A duvet of garnet, topaz and gold
Mother Earth adorns herself proud and bold.

The Hudson reflects the Catskill's trees
A dappled mirror image, if you please
An empirical metamorphisis
Emoting a cornucopia of bliss.

Like linens from the line, crisp and clean
Warm sun and chilled air feels pristine
Just as a grist wheel, seasons must turn
Autumn falls to winter and warmth we yearn.

The change is inevitable we know
Fallen leaves covered with a quilt of snow
But this too, will change as seasons do
The only constant is change, we ensue.

Trail of Fears

A proud people, the Cherokee
Forced from their land, forced to flee
Empty promises and little more
No idea what was in store

Diseased blankets they were given
Mile after mile they were driven
So many perished walking the trail
It wasn't for the old or the frail

Never again would it be the same
From lush forests to the plain
A river cried with their silent tears
But they pushed forth on this trail of fears

It is said on this trail a flower grows
Fertilized from tears, the Cherokee Rose
For every soul lost along the way
A blossom flourished 'til this day...

The Witches Creed

Ghouls and goblins roam street to street
Each in hopes for something sweet
Witches won't be flying o'er head
It's the eve we honor the dead

The altar decked with gourds and fruit
A cauldron seethes with herbs and root
The elements called; earth, water, fire, air
Frankincense and myrrh not to spare

The Sabbath Samhain or Halloween
Filters the realms of in between
The veil thins for them to arrive
Ethereal ancestors do contrive

With an athame the circle's cast
All are in, present and past
Invited spirits we ingratiate
All together we celebrate

Dancing and chanting to raise energy
Invoking the Goddess to oversee
Do what ye will, yet ye harm none
The witches creed, said and spun...

Game of Life

Constant abuse, she could not endure
Murder, her final option to explore
Crimson alchemy would surely flood
With decadent images of his blood

No remorse nor sorrow was ever felt
A royal flush, not the hand 'twas dealt
Too much to sacrifice in this game
It truly was a crying shame

No one found his missing corpse
In the asylum she further warps
Guilty as charged from a jury of peers
Her mind incarcerated all these years

Phantoms and demons plague her brain
Oblivious of sin, she's so insane
Fog so thick it could be cut by knife
Locked away, her sentence is life...

In Vain

The bloody massacre occurred this night
A plethora of men lost their fight
While others writhe in dismal pain
They fought hard but all in vain

Flood waters washed away their sin
Baptizing souls that lied within
Circumstances unusual at best
Innocents lost may never rest

In the distance a virgin wades
Making no sense of the eve's crusades
Anguished and full of utter disgust
Crimson tides in honor of her trust

Her true love lost this fateful night
His intentions were pure and so right
Father learned their secret to wed
Now her intended lies with the dead

In the shadows observing his daughter
As she wanders about in red water
In his victory everything lost
The father's daughter too high a cost...

Golden Cage

Love in my life clearly I miss
Maybe you'll be my last first kiss
I quiver from your tender caress
Putty in your hands, I do confess

I feel comfort knowing you are there
Bliss with you I would love to share
There's nothing like the honeymoon stage
Like an exotic bird in a golden cage

Judgment or discern, not thus far
The way I feel is way over par
In your eyes will I see a future?
Or will my heart need another suture?

If I should fall, I pray to be caught
A soft landing is all that's sought
Are you the one to tear down the wall?
My hearts barricade yearns to fall

If it's not to be, I will survive
Alone once more, a love deprived
An open door on the golden cage
Another chapter, turn the page…

Nothing Left

A satin pillow for my head
For some reason they believe me dead
Can't move, not even blink an eye
But hear everything, I wonder why

My children here, softly they speak
Many questions, answers they seek
Tender sobs, nothing left to do
An ugly riddle and not one clue

So dark in here blacker then coal
No vitals, yet still have my soul
"I'm alive", I scream in my head
Unheard words and tears I can't shed

Panic quickens, there's no way out
I'm not dead, what's this all about?
Lower and lower, six feet under
No hope, I am left asunder

Horrific noise, clanging, banging, crash
Twisted mind, memories I rehash
Blind, burning silence deafens my ear
Madness succumbs, nothing left to fear

The Reaper shows his evil mask
A job to do, he completes his task
Reaching out, he offers his hand
Time is up, I now understand...

Desire

Smooth, body of an hourglass,
enmeshed in desire,
enticing, titillating,
tantalizing,
stimulate me
like no other,
your slave to command,
take me, I'm forever yours...

The Edge of Night

Welcomed you with an open heart
Open arms from the very start
Invited us to a bountiful feast
A cornucopia, to say the least

Gain our trust then stab our back
Stolen land and under attack
Sinister motives, shame on you
Cherokee, Blackfoot, even Sioux

Heathen, savage or wild beast
No respect to say the least
Marching us up the "Trail of Tears"
Unknown certainty causing fears

You tried to break us, steal our light
Proud people on the edge of night
Broken promises, fractured trust
No matter what, we would not rust

Beware of wolves dressed as sheep
Keep one eye open in your sleep
Whatever happens, guard your heart
Don't put horses behind the cart…

Forever After

It's been a week, I can not wait
I truly hope that this is fate
Talking and texting on the phone
I'm getting primed, I'm in the zone

Anticipation is killing me
Pondering on the date to be
Excitement filled like a tot
on Christmas morn' eyeing the lot

Disappointment I do fear
Don't leave me hanging with a tear
Praying you're all you seem to be
Eager to know your thoughts of me

At this moment you appear a catch
Guarded hopes we're a perfect match
A chivalrous soul, my white knight
Riding forth to shine my light

A fairy tale ending I do seek
I will convey, you spark my peak
Are you the one to conquer my heart?
Or, will it again be torn apart?

Star gazing from within your eyes
Hoping not to see my demise
Anticipating love and laughter
In your heart forever after...

Mercenary of Light

Celestial they just might be
Not really meant for us to see
No halo's or harps in hand
Our hardships they understand

Angels walk among us
Might be a stranger on the bus
Be kind to one another, I plead
Could be the sob that you need

At birth we're assigned a fleet
Ethereal beings complete
Free will divides us from the rest
Life lessons to learn from at best

Not all have a beautiful face
Lines of hardship, commonplace
Experience of darker days
Yet glide in light so many ways

What is a light mercenary?
Something we should all query
Could be anyone on the street
Always be kind to those you meet

These beings of light don't involve
But, if it's not our time, they resolve
In God's glory they certainly bask
Yet at our rescue if we ask

On Bated Breath

From afar, what seemed like eternity,
I searched your soul for security.
Did not mean to stare, to gaze.
Your aura cast a brilliant haze.

Lost in your azure eyes at first glance,
silently, I pleaded for a chance.
Like a coward, too shy to verbalize.
Hoping against hope you'd realize.

Captivated by your essence from afar.
Suffocating like a firefly in a jar.
Searching for appropriate words to say,
the message I truly wished to convey.

Finally, on bated breath I said,
"I have tickets to see The Grateful Dead.
I'd be honored if you'd be my date!
My apologies for asking so late..."

The expression on your face spoke volumes.
"You'll pick me up early, I'd assume?"
Our dialog flowed like a mountain creek.
No longer feeling like such a geek...

Three years later, I kick myself for being shy.
"I love you completely", he said with a sigh...

Glen Brook Farm

Have you heard the legend of that farm?
It's Glen Brook, down the lane on the right.
Years ago, the family endured fatal harm,
spite and vengeance on the fateful night.

Standing soldiers awaiting winters death.
Bare limbs blanketed with heavy snow.
Hid within, cold enough to see his breath,
awaiting opportunity to close the show.

He, a hired hand, lost his job New Year's eve.
Given months notice of his final day,
a resentful plan went up his sleeve.
Gruesome details of how they'd pay.

Glen Brook Farm, fallen on hard times,
as they often do in the dead of winter.
Proud family blind to the hand's design,
paralyzed by fear as the air splinters.

The trio arrived from evening mass.
Unsuspected evil hid among those trees.
Stifling sounds of gunshot breaking glass.
Prisoners of war upon bended knees.

One by one, executed in their home.
The last round was saved for his head.
Rumor has it their specters do roam,
and there's crimson stains from where they bled.

Unholy terror raged that holiday.
Annual shots heard from miles around.
It happens without fail, is what they say,
and four souls wander the Glen Brook ground...

A New Chapter Reigns

Once again, a special time of year,
raise your stein to Ra, and spread good cheer!
Pagans chant and dance all in good fun,
celebrating the brilliant, almighty sun...

Insuperable importance, this light
life without insufferable night.
Folk exist in continuous fear,
trying to cope this way year after year...

Birth, death, rebirth, a new chapter reigns.
The horizon red, but not with blood stains.
The utmost succinct calender day.
Rendering time for party and play.

Luminosity thrives more and more,
from the heartland to our every shore.
At least in the northern hemisphere,
the pagans circle is cast with cheer!

Winter Solstice, the most revered day.
More then celebrating, it's life's way,
such beauty, it is breathtaking.
In reality, it is earth shaking....

A few moments here, and also there,
adding up daily, 'til there's time to spare.
Incandescence shining refulgence;
Hope is alive in great resplendence!

Fade

So many flashing lights in the driveway
Everyone squealing, but can't hear what they say
They load you in the ship, I catch your eye
Pleading, begging, screaming asking why...

It's all too familiar, but a lifetime ago
Just a child then, tell me it's not so
Ravished by fever, no promises made
"He'll be comfortable, but it will fade..."

All I could do was reach for my "friend"
Thinking this could easily be your end
Find the vein, let me off of this ride
I feel the pin, the works, true and tried

What a frightful night, they've called the time
Too young, you haven't even hit your prime
Life and death, so heartless and cruel
Not the lessons we were taught in school

I need a corner, somewhere to tie the knot
Heat the spoon, cook the rest of what I've got
Give me the pin, it's all over, it's done
I... Have become, comfortably numb....

Hung With Care...

Two by two just like Noah's ark
Couples everywhere do embark
Beaming in the jewelry store
Shiny diamonds gleam some more

No rationale to chop down a tree
Yuletide for the squirrels, not for me
No garland nor stockings hung with care
Perhaps from lights, I'll rig a snare

Me and the cat alone for Christmas
My boys, spending it with their Mrs.
No Santa nor reindeer, not even an elf
Rum and eggnog to drink by myself

The grand kids all live so far away
No joyful laughter as they run and play
So quiet the noise deafens my ears
Drink another to wash down the tears

Not so much as a mistletoe kiss
At least a week before I'll be missed
Bring the New Year in with a hell of a bang
Twinkling white lights from where I hang...

If I Were You…

My dear children, I must bid you adieu
Millenniums have passed, all for you
Lacking for nothing, always wanting more
You're spoiled rotten, right to the core

Still question if you evolved from the apes
Creatures to amuse you, all sizes and shapes
Food bountiful, a cornucopia of flavor
Because I love you, and I'm your savior

Amazing scenery, something for each taste
You trashed it, everything in haste
Once it was beautiful, now it's all gone
Please tell me, where did I go wrong?

The indigenous people had it from go
Love the land, and reap what you sow
Never take more then you will need
Others came, filled with so much greed

I have given you so many warnings
Even as simple as global warming
Selfish, hateful, greedy with power lust
I remember teaching you of love and of trust

This is the end for me, it's my demise
I can't stand to hear the pleas and the cries
Enough is too much, I'm over the edge
Can't listen to another empty pledge

Do not cry for me when I am no longer
Help your brother, make yourself stronger
To err is human, to forgive divine
I've done my part, now it's my time

As you read this, it'll be way too late
What will you do with this kind of fate?
Can you survive, or will you die too?
Changes would be made, if I were you

Stop the world, I'm at the end of my rope
It's all over, I can no longer cope
Good luck to you, remember your free will
How much more blood is there left to spill?

I loved you all, each one as an equal
But the movie's over, there is no sequel
I leave you now, with a wink and a nod
My love to you,

"Your Almighty God"

Without You (a Kyrielle Sonnet)

Thank you for watching over me
Your face I would prefer to see
Nothing is the same without you
Christmas is so lonely and blue...

Evergreens have lost their luster
Decorating I can't muster
Caroler's seem to be off cue
Christmas is so lonely and blue...

It's better to give than receive
Something you taught me to believe
You held us together; the glue
Christmas is so lonely and blue...

Thank you for watching over me
Christmas is so lonely and blue...

Hummingbird Tears

Joyful resonance
swaying, flirting,
dancing upon
a summer's breeze.
Each conduit,
it's own life.
Stringed structure
tuned to the ear
of an angel.
So melodious,
bringing tears of joy
to hummingbirds.
Charming and
elegant,
reminding me
of Sprites, flitting about
on a summer's morn,
as they trip the light fandango...

Your Center

Sadness, happiness,
soulfulness or shy.
Always telling a story,
the way of your eyes.
A window to the soul
is what's always said.
Those azure beauties
put women to bed.
Young and devilish
or wizened from age,
your center being
of this earthly stage.
Celestial or terrestrial,
my favorite gauge...

My Darkened Doorway

Menacing dark clouds loom overhead
They appear to ensue, no matter what
Often perplexed to how I arise from bed
Why the bad karma? I'm not some harlot!

My life auspicious, malignant at best.
Joy has been taken, no reason to smile.
Nerves warped, anxiety ridden, such a test.
It's off the hook, no longer worthwhile.

Nobody to turn to, no one has my back.
Dependability, a word from the past.
Totally alone, except while under attack.
Amazing just how long pain can last.

Evil entities? None that I can see.
Love is gone, uncomparably remote.
My darkened doorway, black as night can be.
Desolate and forlorn, with a heart to devote.

Have I been cursed, or is this a wicked spell?
Am I haunted by demons? Already stranded in hell...

In the Name of Love…

Another day you want to slit your throat
In the name of "love" with no heart to devote
Constant reminder of being alone
Deafening noise of an unringing phone

My best friend since I can first remember
It was third grade, the ninth of December
Flag football at recess that chilly day
Wanting to speak, but there's nothing to say

I was bullied for hanging with the guys
You stuck up for me, much to my surprise
I was atop the world that afternoon
So many ups and downs started real soon

That was thirty years ago, it went fast
'Til today, then here comes the ugly past
Watching you buy roses for another
Felt like taking a blade to my juglar

A plethora of thoughts racing my mind
Husband and dad, is that how you're defined?
I've got your whole evening planned for you
Dinner, with dessert to go, for two

Dainty, pink rose petals to lead the way
You must've planned this for many a day
White candle flames dance in your big, bright, blues
How much you love her, you've left all the clues

A single tear, the one I couldn't hold
Rolls down my cheek, where it's starting to fold
Almost got married once but you were present
In my heart, I couldn't keep you dormant

Another Valentine's Day all alone
Nothing changed except I'll turn off the phone
Put my pajamas on, order food in
Shed some tears for the way it could've been...

Your Loss, Not Mine...

One's reflection is not who they are
Life is challenging enough as it is
Especially when you aren't the star
Look deep, that's where you'll find bliss

I have aged like the finest of wine
and wizened like the Great Horned Owl
My clothing is a different design
none of which makes me fair or foul

Ponder deeply into my hazel eyes
Feel the warmth from within my heart
This is where actual radiance lies
Beauty is cultivated from the start

Not everyone is born pretty faced
Yet can light an entire room
It's not the container ones encased
Often weeds have the most vibrant bloom

I've become a woman over time
Lines on my face, curves on my hips
The grace I've lost isn't a crime
Honey still seeps from my heart shaped lips

I'm not the girl I used to be
Now I spend each weekend all alone
Someone is missing out on my sincerety
While seeking out my teenage clone

I say it's your loss, it's not mine
You wade in very shallow water
And would only be a waste of time
I'm many things, but not out of order!

Transcend

Ominous and deep, obsidian black
A creature of cultivated mystery
Revered, yet not none for attack
'Til recently, this has been it's history

A wizard of old lived in the wood
The onyx bird attacked at whim
Why, the alchemist has not understood
The magic man angry, filled to the brim

Normally, the raven is a bird of day
Not one to be a burden at night; a lark
Why this is, I can't truthfully say
Maybe they are "blind" in the dark

Hidden in murky shadows, he attacks with force
Infuriating the wizard, fighting his foe
A shape-shifter perhaps, running his course
The old man would die before letting secrets go

Gathering the ingrediants in need
Calling upon ancestors long past dead
He'd put a stop to this at once, indeed
Cunning and wily, this wizard is said

Without killing, he chose to fix him for good
He spell cast, turning the raven blood red
Proud as a peacock, the crimson bird stood
The alchmist felt defeated,as the raven difiantely stood

The Blood Raven was a sight for sore eyes to see
Spells had never backfired in the past

This one didn't either, the bird left him be
But the other ravens thought he was a minion; aghast

A product of an old wizard's magic
Maybe the Blood Raven lost all friends
To many, this would be sorrowful; tragic
The blood stained raven now free to transcend

Victorious were both in the very end
The bird left, leaving the antiquated wizard be
No injuries to either, a case to defend
As the Thunderbird, the Blood Raven rose mightily!

'No One Rides for Free'

If I could time travel, back to the '70's I'd go
Especially if I knew, what I now know
A careless stoner, anything to get high
Whatever it takes, said with a sigh

Purple Microdot, opium, 'shrooms, THC
Magical, mystical, the definition of free
Seconds were hours, how time would fly
Everything was funny, but no one knew why

Skipping school with every opportunity
Load up my "bucket", and off we'd be
Jethro Tull, or Led Zep blaring
Singing along, so bold and daring

No disco for me, rock all the way
The louder the better, what can I say?
It was an era for sex, drugs and rock and roll
Sooner or later, it would take it's toll

"Ass, gas or grass, no one rides for free"
There was always a price, always a fee
As the ride on River Styx, the price was high
Many succumbed, no one's friend should die

If I had another chance, I think I'd study more
I partied way too much, that is for sure
No recollection of scholarships for a perfect joint
But if you never let loose, what the hell is the point?

T.I.M.E.

The time is very soon
My life I've lived, I must go
If cordially granted one last wish
Let each dwell in their own shadow

Please quench my thirst, I appeal to you
A lot to ask of your authority
I plead in behalf of our children
They must be taught capability

Cease encroachment on everyone
Children and creatures are innocent
Deserving to reside in harmony
Enlighten them to become valiant

Appropriate our baby's fears
Trepidition engages conflict
Combat is never the answer
World peace, the only verdict

Equality is the resolution
Leading by example, the best way
It'll take time: T.hings I. M.ust E.arn
A powerful message to convey

I have but one wish to be granted
But covers a vast domain
Mother Earth has endured too much
Future minds must be engrained...

Not in the Cards...

After her tarot reading
Jill never arrived at work
The boss tried contacting her
Losing it, going berserk

Jill's lifeless body was found
Strangled along the bike trail
Her boyfriend was arrested
But was later out on bail

Few were investigated
The tarot reader was next
Though she didn't have answers,
she read for them at request

The cards denoted Jill's love
Further interrogation
He was found to have motive
But solid affirmation

Unfaithful, not a killer
Seen around with another
A woman from out of town
The mystic's estranged mother

The other woman so jealous
She wanted him all alone
Calculating and concise
But her alibi came unsewn...

Looking Out

Through my kitchen window
The world swiftly glides by
Appreciating birds
Nourishing their supply

Replenishing feeders
Their fuel when it's cold
In turn, they despense joy
With hues vividly bold

Winged beings astonish
Pigments of a rainbow
Diminutive footprints
In opalescent snow...

Free Me

Why her and why not me?
She's a mere fantasy
With blinded eyes you see
Not a good thing will be
You just think you're free
It's bonded slavery
You'll pay up dearly
Soul mates eternally
You claimed we'd always be
I cry so audibly
Release these tears freely
My love, I give to thee
I do so faithfully,
also passionately,
with deep intensity.
It's a mere casualty
Never was meant to be...

No Remorse

In the abyss of my being
Darkness shrouds my weakened soul
Obscurity of happiness
Deflected my heart into coal
No longer do I dwell in sun
Now encompassed by the night
Surviving mortality
Inpenetrable from light
Mysterious, undisclosed
Unilluminated course
This shadowy path I choose
Sacrilegious, no remorse...

The Field

The last warrior prowls the field
All dead beneath their broken shield
Out numbered, but they wouldn't yield
Wives became widows on this day
Wailing over men where they lay

The warrior's wraith can't be still
He lead his soldiers up that hill
Guilty of the graves they now fill
Always seen in his bloody clothes
His purgatory, I suppose

No one has ever seen his face
Merely an ethereal trace
Yet always around the same place
The spot the canon was once wheeled
The last warrior prowls the field...

*Death is not the end to be feared or to be cried over, but a new
beginning in which to celebrate.*

Critters Melody,

Pretty brunette, green eyes
Mother Earth's little prize
Snow flurries in the air
Not a want, nor a care
Nature girl all the way
Her fiddle she loves to play
Woodland critters gather 'round
Come to hear her magic sound
Just as happy as can be
Playing the Critters Melody

Day of Vows

A day of vows, her dreams shattered
Thinking love was all that mattered
Her lovely gown torn and tattered
Caught her intended with a man
She's not a prude, but not a fan

Her life carries on, his did not
He had never seen her this hot
No wedding, but she tied the knot
Around his neck the rope did go
Chopped off his penis, all for show

This isn't how life was to be
Cheating on her in secrecy
She took delight hearing his plea
All the while his blood splattered
A day of vows, her dreams shattered...

Goddess Bast

Egyptian Goddess Bast
Please watch over this rite
Your coat, obsidian sky
This extraordinary night
With your amber cat eye
'til Ra shows his first light
Your protection we rely...

Evil Night

―――・◈・―――

Evil lurks his benighted mind
Demonic ways, one of a kind
The ways of light, this creature's blind

Sunshine causes pain, it's too bright
Straight from Hell, he emotes true fright
This entity is not contrite

Sinister serial killer found
Nefariousness can't be bound
Exaggerated imp astounds

Contamination

---◈◈---

Dissolution is all around
A web-like substance can be found
Malignancy that's so unsound
What perversity could occur?
A malicious debauched monster

The prophetess spoke of this night
Saw it all in her second sight
With awareness, she saw the plight
The population scoffed at her
No one listened to the augur

Other worldly devastation
Such depraved annihilation
With a complete termination
This contamination's profound
Dissolution is all around

Memories

Insidious nightmares invade my sleep
An evil presence, I can't make a peep
Hidden in shadows, I am tempting fate
The "monster" is someone I know and hate

Painful memories, I am dripping wet
Soaking sheets with hot flashes and cold sweat
Ominous feelings have terrified me
The dark side of the moon is all I can see

Haunting visions of a sinister time
In these bleakest moments, I am defined
Malevolent ideas run away
Severe depression, decadent dismay...

Unaccepted

Panic, terror, and anxiety
Unaccepted in society
They keep you frozen in your place
Make it so you won't show your face
Debilitating painfully
I must shake it off to be free

Steal Away

---◈◈---

The world can be cold as ice
Memories that aren't so nice
Alcohol and drugs I tried
Temporary to be fried
Sleep is my latest avenue
It's the escape I pursue
Dream away all my worry
It can't be harmful, surely
Steal away from reality
Allow another side of me...

Testimony

Your testimony will convict
You will have a guilty verdict
A maniac you do depict
States evidence turned the table
Certainly you are unstable

Your guilt, obvious as a duck
Left your fingerprints on the truck
So much blood for a sawbuck
Tried saying you weren't capable
Put your horse back in the stable

Data was strictly compiled
Everything ready for trial
Now you can watch the clocks dial
It was such a bloody conflict
Your testimony will convict

All the Same

You took my heart, you had it all
Like a drug, you were my downfall
I've been in it for the long haul

Things went south, they went about face
Feelin' like I'm in outer-space
Don't really think I like this place

I'm bludgeoned, bruised but still standing
Boy, you are way too demanding
I was in for a crash landing

Stole my heart then tossed it away
You aren't the man you once portrayed
You're a dirty dog, a filthy stray

Need ONE to prove you're not all the same
To be the one that you proclaim
It truly is a crying shame...

Caged

I took a bite that changed my life
With inner anguish, guilt and strife
Never again will I be free
A monstrous werewolf lives in me

I thought this was fake, all folk lore
I've been bit, nothing to explore
Shackled and caged for your safety
A monstrous werewolf lives in me

Evilness courses through my veins
It makes me mad, feeling insane
Just a creature chasing query
A monstrous werewolf lives in me

I took a bite that changed my life
A monstrous werewolf lives in me

On the Lam

The "heats" directly on my tail
Need to get the scent off my trail
I'll have to hit a bank for bail
Now a fugitive on the lam
No time to chat, I have to scram

Wanted to go for a joy ride
Found this beauty on the curbside
Now there's a search for me statewide
Get the hell out of my way, ma'am
I have to get with the program

I really don't want to get caught
If only I had a forethought
Hopefully, a cop can be bought
Now I can hear the sirens wail
The "heats" directly on my tail

The Debauched Queen

The debauched queen has lost her head
Her reign's over because she's dead
Dementia brought the queen down
Quite a spectacle for the town

Her bastard son wanted to be king
Madness is a family thing
Dipped his mothers face in the wax
Melted half off and now it slacks

The son had her quartered and drawn
What a sinister, bastard spawn
Revenge is best when it's served cold
She haunted him 'til he was old

In the dungeon she would appear
His expression locked; face of fear
Her reign's over because she's dead
The debauched queen has lost her head!

Enough

Maybe not today, nor tomorrow
You're going to end my sorrow
I won't be just another body
Or a bloody curiosity
I'll be enough for you
You'll want to pursue

Touchdown

---◆⟨♦⟩◆---

The wizened detective took the case
Small girl found with a bludgeoned face
Born and raised in this red-necked town
He'd run the field until his touchdown

Follow each lead 'til the bitter end
Now and then the law was meant to bend
This seasoned gumshoe would find his clown
He'd run the field until his touchdown

The local-yokels helped where they could
Questioning everyone as they should
A confession came from Mr. Brown
He'd run the field until his touchdown

The wizened detective took the case
He'd run the field until his touchdown

Dad

Your birthday was just last week
Your aroma I still seek
If I could just hear you speak

Almost four years have gone by
I still get tears in my eye
There's no way to say goodbye

I hold you in high esteem
Your eyes always had a gleam
So glad I'm from your bloodstream...

Serenity

Hermit teaches acceptance and time
Hard lessons to learn but not a crime
Patience is a double edged sword
Acceptance and time or there's discord

The Hermit's wise and becomes serene
It's not all at once he starts out green
To learn to accept one must submit
Time alone teaches how to commit

When Hermit shows up you should retreat
Time to learn his ways, to be complete
Get comfortable in your own skin
Important changes start to begin

You're not left in dark, he has light
His lantern illuminates quite bright
Over time you'll learn what you need
Study his knowledge, you will succeed...

The Fiddle

Along the shore late each night
Play my fiddle out of sight
Just me and Grandmother Moon
At times, I'll even croon
Darkness washes over me
Hiding what you needn't see

My verse and the pounding waves
Haunting pleasure from deep graves
Swells oscillate dampened stones
Reminds me of crackling bones
Reverberate to unite
Along the shore, late each night

Dark, slate clouds conceal the stars
There's no way to hide my scars
The fiddle drowns out my pain
Otherwise, I'd go insane
Evenin' tunes suffer this plight
Along the shore, late each night...

Heated Desire

He played all night with heated desire
The only light, candlelit fire
Driving him mad to a frenzied thirst
Some thought him gifted, but he was cursed

Handsome, eloquent, forever young
Beautifully spoken, silver tongue
Always donned in finest attire
He played all night with heated desire

That fateful bite, many moons ago
At first so sick, then he was aglow
Music he sincerely aspired
He played all night with heated desire

The violin was his saving grace
Though evilness he could not embrace
Incessant, he'd never retire
He played all night with heated desire...

I Dream...

Out the window, neon light shines
Frosted panes obscure the white pines
Resting on the sofa, I dream
A bright kaleidoscope moonbeam

Celestial reflections dance
Crossing with Milky Way romance
Everything meets, sky to shorelines
Out the window, neon light shines

Straight from literature books
Flying the heavens, onyx rooks
Following ethereal lines
Out the window, neon light shines

So tranquil in the land of nod
Everything appears a bit odd
But, at least there are no deadlines
Out the window, neon light shines...

Weeping Willow

A lone blossom in a flower bed
Alabaster skin and ginger-head
Radiance shines forth her silhouette
Cascading shadows with the sunset

A Weeping Willow among the oak
A delicate lover whom's heart broke
Too many tears this woman has bled
A lone blossom in a flower bed

Sorrow permeates her soft shoulder
No longer is she a hard boulder
Too much has gone by and left unsaid
A lone blossom in a flower bed

Emotional currents are output
Saline streams nourish blossoms afoot
Further suffering she needs to shed
A lone blossom in a flower bed...

Solitare

Pain's too great won't take anymore
Can't even bare to see the shore
The sunny brilliance burns my eyes
Empower the leap to demise

Enough is too much I beg of thee
My final vision aqua sea
No longer do I feel your touch
Cleave unto you, this heart is such

Spending my world in solitaire
Their sole purpose is so unfair
Extending a hand, none reach back
My whole life was under attack

The sorrow has depleted me
From this anguish I must be free
Loveless life is no life at all
It's time to jump before I fall...

Tragic

A fateful day in September
Places always remember
The world lost it's mind that day
People all over had to pray

A worldwide collision hit home
Rubble, cadavers and bent chrome
Still receiving bags we don't want
Tragic times forever do haunt

The Fey

At the passing of each busy day
Aside my hollow to view their play
Intoxicating, forest bouquet
Illuminating sky are the fey

Welcome nymphs and fireflys singing
Tiny voices and bells are ringing
It's remarkable in the airway
Illuminating sky are the fey

Mushroom rings and ivy deck my tree
A very magical place to be
An enchanting forest, the forte'
Illuminating sky are the fey

At the end of a long, busy day
Illuminating sky are the fey

My Hunger

I am Lamia
Here to consume your tot
Voracious for your unborn
You shall be sacrificed
I will gorge upon your fetus
Sucking the meat from
His drumsticks
Then and only then
My insatiable hunger
Will be fulfilled...

Pink Ruffles

Pink ruffles frame her tiny face
Golden hair not one out of place
She's picture perfect every way
There is no exception today

Like a lily among the weeds
Little droplets of dewy beads
She's standing tall with so much grace
Pink ruffles frame her tiny face

Silky smooth in a rock garden
Such beauty never a bargain
No blemishes never a trace
Pink ruffles frame her tiny face

Listen

As my words
resonate
in your ears,
I plead with you,
feel them
in your heart
and allow them
to reside in
your soul...

Whispers

The center of my Milky Way
Amazing things you used to say
The ways you pretended to be
Was not life's reality

Whispers of a fairy tale life
Wasted years, your devoted wife
I tossed aside my finest years
At your side but shedding tears

The only vice I could not kick
Despising you, yet still love sick
Addicted to you from the start
Eternal control of my heart

I had the same affect on you
Back together out of the blue
Stronger then a magnetic force
Love sickness the evil source

Under the sheet your lifeless face
You had just arrived from my place
The only vow you didn't bend
Together at the very end

Divorced yet forever married
My name in ink you still carried
Now a junkie without my fix
Saline rivers through the lyrics

No more whispers of fairy tales
Yet, in my heart your love prevails
Destined to spend my life alone
I beg my God to bring me home...

Burn

I was yours from the very start
Captivated my starving heart
Now you're gone never to return
Took your own life, time to burn

Stood at your side all of those years
Licking my wounds and wiping tears
I couldn't compete your mistress
And you could not keep a promise

Alcohol was your number one
Although it was no longer fun
The last destination you were bound
My name went with you into the ground

The tale over, no fairy's found
Rivers I've cried have no sound
Now you're gone never to return
Took your own life, time to burn...

Death's Door

Alone she awaits at death's door
She's got a new realm to explore
Never has she been anyone's fool
Although, she's known many a ghoul

Just inside the hell-hounds await
The true guardians of the gate
Reaper already claimed her soul
Her name at the top of the scroll

Luna is full over her head
Befitting to cover the dead
Sprites fly over unhallowed ground
Maybe spirits whom are heaven bound

Blood stained tears against china skin
What was this Gothic beauty's sin?
Did she kill her love in the act?
Something she can never retract...

Shadow Gazing

The spell cast, everyone's gone home
Me and my familiar are all alone
Gazing upon shadows being cast
Light of the full moon will not last

Candle smoke rising to the sky
Bats overhead make an eerie cry
Ominously flying to the Belfast
In my dark thoughts they trespass

Goddess Isis do you hear my plea?
Please forgive that I burden thee
Circle is over the spell to Bast
Now it's behind me, kept in my past

Gazing upon shadows being cast
Light of the full moon will not last...

Divine Vows

Whether Samhain or Halloween
An eve the veil thins in between
Ethereal ancestors come through
A major sabot and "I do"

The pagan couple hand-fasting
May their love be everlasting
Fire, water, earth and air
Watchful guardians will be there

A sacred circle shall be cast
The couple join the priest long last
Silver linings and golden bands
Silken chords shall bind their hands

Divine vows of love and trust
Promises to discern beyond the rust
Witnessed by friends and family
This rite attained, so mote it be!

Deprivation

Alone in bed, late each night
I hear the whispers, such a fright
Keep on searching but out of sight
Making me crazy with all their might

I haven't slept for so very long
Get out of my head, just be gone
Deprivation is running strong
I have no clue what's right or wrong

Sanity has escaped from me
I'm held hostage, no longer free
Is there an entity I can't see?
No more fooling with the ouija

I hear the whispers, such a fright
Alone in bed, late each night
I haven't slept for so very long
Deprivation is running strong...

A Welcomed Sight

A has-been poet lost his muse
Trying to write but what's the use
Maybe a nap, he takes a snooze
Crazy nightmares, his new excuse

Deadlines looming, he makes a pact
No way out, he can not retract
He has signed the Devil's contract
Yet to realize the full impact

With a demon yelling in his ear
This situation beyond austere
His hand's trembled, so full of fear
He's trekking through a new frontier

To the left another voice is heard
Instead of yelling, it whispered
Thereupon, he sat and pondered
Who would believe, it's so absurd

Finally, he opt for the light
His only hope, with the pact airtight
The muse back, now able to write
Seeing the angel, a welcomed sight

Good versus evil, there's no match
An army of angels were dispatched
All negativity he detached
Starting over, starting from scratch...

A Snail's Pace

Here upon my toadstool I do sit
A moth flies near with lantern lit
Not a typical leprechaun, I admit
Though mom was a fae, I'm legit

Time is moving at a snails pace
That's why I wear a grimace upon my face
I'm so old I'd like time to efface
Pack it all away in an old suitcase

Not exactly what one would call cute
Like other's dressed up in their green suit
My nose and feet are long like snakeroot
Given my own horn I dare not toot

St. Pat's day is just around the bend
Another holiday to contend
I'll paint a smile on and pretend
This is time I'd love to transcend

Living in shadows of nature's face
My forest home is a real showplace
Beneath this toadstool is my birthplace
Time is moving at a snails pace...

Fate Was Sealed

Late at night he listens to her scream
Praying it's just one horrific dream
Hearing the Banshee is an ominous sign
A hag wanting your soul is her design

An eerie sound echoes through the dale
Urban legend or perhaps a tall tale
When you're cognizant of her late at night
Then it becomes one hell of a fright

Rumors declare if you see her, time draws near
She'll come to your bed, paralyzing with fear
Sucking out your life force 'til you're dead
Imagine rising to the hag while asleep in bed

The legend originated from Emerald Isle
Variations have been passed for quite awhile
Wherever she is, this hag is deadly
No escape from the wails of the Banshee

Satan's minion or an entity flying solo?
I predict it's too late before you'll know
At the pub he tells his mates this ordeal
Later that night the man's fate was sealed

A dark wraith now roams the castle ground
Some believe he is eternally bound
Praying it's just one horrific dream
Late at night listening to the Banshee scream...

Unspoken Love

My tiny babe I prayed for thee
Highest blessing awarded me
I promise to always be there
At your side with loving care
Priceless gift from above
Declarations unspoken love...

Lady In the Lake

This beauty is The Lady in the Lake
She's quite powerful, make no mistake
On this day while taking a break
She noticed an odd thing, a tiny baby drake

Nourishment and love is what the dragon needs
Unsure of herself, she gets juice from milkweeds
Please drink little one, the Lady doth pleads
Without hesitation the dragon concedes

Pleased as punch The Lady is with her pet
But worries the dragon's mom will be really upset
She builds a fire for warmth right at sunset
Used to the water, she gained quite a sweat

It was the dragon The Lady worried for
He was a strong one so she named him Thor
By morning light the two had a tight rapport
She had to look for his mama, and went to explore

This beauty is The Lady in the Lake
She noticed an odd thing, a tiny baby drake...

On My Own...

The only constant in my world
Just as the rising sun,
I could count upon you
In just one breath, gone...
Saline rivers, white water rapids
Saturating my downy pillow
Tumultuous, heaving sobs
A hurricane of grief
With no end in sight...
So many storms we weathered
You, the bridge I often needed
I'm left to search for the sun
For dry land, for refuge,
Isolated and on my own....
My rock, I leaned upon you
Now shattered, mere pebbles
Will I be able to stand?
Isolated and on my own...

Hell In the Hallway

A light at the end of the hallway
That's really an old, used cliche'
A spirit waiting to ruin your day
Feel the goosebumps just about midway?

Is it malicious, or perhaps benign?
I dare you, go ask it for a sign
When the warmth escapes from sunshine
And cold chills scramble up your spine

All those footsteps you hear overhead
Late night trying to sleep in your bed
Giving you feelings of fright and dread
In that corridor is the walking dead

One door closes, one opens they say
But it's always hell in the hallway
Personally, I wouldn't delay
Not when it's haunted by some hombre'...

I Fear...

---◦❨◦❩◦---

Though no stranger, I fear pain
The deep, vast abyss of being lonely
Misunderstood,
Unaccepted,
Neglected,
Like a Leper without a colony
I wear my heart upon my sleeve
Around it, an impenetrable fortress
With a mote full of crocodilian
Patrolled by fire-breathing dragons
A living, breathing contradiction
Finding solace in my solitude
Free of demands,
Of commitment
I fear being lonely
But not of being alone
Of dying
But not death
I am an enigma
A paradox
I fear...

Sweet Serendipity

A gentle glimmer in his eyes
A creased brow renders him wise
Ingesting honesty, no hidden lies
Definitely not her final demise

Not a predator, nor is she prey
His aura bright, not mottled grey
Rugged and successful, that's his way
Leaving work behind when it's time to play

She can't avoid getting lost in his gaze
A child-like wonder he easily displays
Captivated by his tender praise
Demolishing walls with an easy craze

Life became sweet serendipity
Quieting voices from her head's committee
No longer thriving alone in self-pity
Her inner-child skips through the big city

For once in her life, she's finally free
Committed to love and to life's mystery
Unshackled from her walls, from her misery
Skip the light fandango, swing from a tree!

Sealed With a Kiss...

Off in the distance there's a grumble
Closer yet, thunder rolls and rumbles
Tension builds, electric in the air
Lightning strikes, take cover, beware

The honeymoon stage is running dry
Isolated from all who might pry
You're ignorant and ugly too
Just ask him, he's the best you can do

Confidence and self-worth are gone
Pushing and shoving before too long
Nursing a shiner, next on the list
A punching bag to his angry fist

"Never again, I promise you this
Please forgive me" sealed with a kiss
For awhile it's like your honeymoon
Don't blink, it'll be over soon

"I've never hit a woman before
You make me do this, stupid whore
Never again, I promise you this
Please forgive me", sealed with a kiss

It's never easy to get away
"She must like it" some will convey
Run and hide for your precious life
Never again a battered wife...

Book of Shadows

—◦◦◦—

Your Book of Shadows left in plain sight
Now it'll be one magical night
Within the coven, I wonder your plight

Energy builds as I chant the spell
The power within, too soon to tell
Perhaps a demon conjured straight from Hell

I feel intensity in the air
Your neglect will leave you solitaire
Be careful they don't cut off your hair

Damage to be done with your book in tow
Karma in jeopardy, keep yourself low
Get it together, all ducks in a row

Tempting it is, I can't keep the book
I know you're scared, can see you're shook
Won't say a word after just one last look

Your Book of Shadows left behind
To anyone this is a great find
Take my advice, cast a spell to bind!

Still Haunted...

When the medics revealed your lifeless face
So much blood, more than just a small trace
Questions running rampant through my brain
Is this a nightmare or have I gone insane?

I went to bed alone that fateful night
Your inebriation gave me a fright
Your mother called early the next morning
You were dead from taking my pills, a warning

Looked like a Disco with all those flashing lights
I answered questions and waited for my rights
A bottle of Morphine missing from my home
Did you take them all and then go roam?

Still haunted by your lifeless, bloodied face
No clue as to what really took place
You were the man I loved more than any other
Too bad you had to deal with your mother

Dead or alive you constantly haunted me
You didn't know how to just leave me be
Now you have an excuse to haunt excessively
Wherever I go, it's your face I always see...

Is it love or a conscience weighed heavily
Not allowing me to live burden free
You're part of the committee in my head
But, I really wish you were not dead...

Powerless and Paralyzed

Filled with horror and with delight
It came to her from in the night
Overcome by this lustful desire
Such intensity, her loins a fire

Was it a dream or a nightmare?
Was she asleep or quite aware?
Was he an angel or demon in guise?
So many questions, knowing it unwise

Riddled with guilt from this passion
Acting out, just not her fashion
She was powerless and paralyzed
An Incubus, she soon realized

He was not ethereal, not at all
She's merely a toy, at his beck and call
Part of this woman-child still confused
How could she enjoy being used?

Overcome by this lustful desire
Such intensity, her loins a fire
Filled with horror and with delight
It came to her from in the night...

Heat of the Night

Heaven and hell
Heat of the night
Such a paradox
Incredible sight
Even the beautiful
Go up in flame
Life or death
Who's to blame?

From the Moon

---◆◈◆---

A sight to behold
For my weary eyes
A translucent face appeared
In the frigid night skies

She was quite celestial
So lovely and elegant
I couldn't help but wonder
Just what was her intent

A vision with delicate features
Among them pointed ears
I was stunned for certain
But put away all fears

She seemed to be crystallized
And dangling from the moon
I found this to be fascinating
Not at all was she jejune

I had been mesmerized
By such a wondrous sight
No way to bat an eyelash
'Til she vanished in the night...

Nature's Harmony

It's a fairy's dream resting aside a stream
A calm, warm breeze, oh so cozy and serene
Thoughts of love caress her mind this joyous day
Wind chimes lull her body into a gentle sway

Scenery reflects in a beautiful, shimmering pool
With a gentle sigh she admires the minnow's school
Life is a like fantasy with angels above you
Birds chirp reminding her of a vision to pursue

Maybe the elves will carve her a wooden flute
There's some in the forest she might recruit
She'll become harmonious and learn to play
Time to put this plan into action without delay

After a few seasons she knows a melody or two
Serenading nature friends without further adieu
Her aspiration has finally come to light
The woodland creatures listen long into the night...

The Fae Hunter

What a horrible, frightening sight
An ogre out fae hunting tonight
He can't stand the twinkle of their light
A true bully, he knows they can't fight

Knowing the fae can fly but not hide
His nasty boar friend at his side
An evil duo, it's bonafide
Neither of which have rules to abide

Tiny wooden cages for the fae
Once caught, it's difficult to get away
He takes their fun, laughter and their play
God forbid, he will probably slay

An ogre out fae hunting tonight
He can't stand the twinkle of their light...